SHOCK WAVES

First published 2012
By the author

http://hanabethluke.tumblr.com
http://www.facebook.com/shock.waves.hanabeth

Foreword by Tim Baker, www.bytimbaker.com.
Cover design by Creative Ink Advertising, www.creativeink.com.au.
Cover images by Alan Williams, Patrick Gorbunovs, Roberto Maldonado
and Simona Satra.
Typesetting by OTTOpia PTY. LTD., ottopia.com.au.

ISBN 978-0-9874081-0-5

SHOCK WAVES

FINDING PEACE AFTER
THE BALI BOMB

by
Hanabeth Luke

This book is dedicated to Marc,
to Tom Singer,
and to Gran.

Also to my family: Mum, Dad, Tommy, Melanie, Lydia,
Dylan, Lian, Jenny, Ian, Julianne, Carole, Ray, Steve,
Catherine and Jonty Marc Gajardo.

It isn't the moment you are struck that you need courage,
but for the long uphill climb back to sanity and
faith and security. – Anne Morrow Lindbergh

Acknowledgements

THIS BOOK WOULD not have happened if it were not for the help, love and efforts of so many people who have supported me through this entire process. Dan Cassidy, I would never have *started* to finish this book without your gentle nudge in October 2011. You've been an incredible friend and inspiration, always.

Tim Baker, without your enthusiasm and heartfelt guidance this book would be twice as long and half as engaging!

Tatiana Velasco, thank you for helping to propel me forwards through this whole process.

Donnie Mc Allister, thank you for creating a beautiful cover, and Kurt Otto, thanks for putting it all together in record time.

Thanks to Simona Satra, Alan Williams, Patrick Gorbunovs, Isabell Heiß and Roberto Maldonado for taking some incredible photos.

Dr David Lloyd, thank you for believing in me.

Without the producers at Tonight with Trevor Macdonald thinking to fly me to London to join the group of extraordinary women, I would never have had the chance to speak with Tony Blair.

The Australian Government continues to support the Australian Bali bomb victims and their families when they need help, and this is much valued.

Jai, I would never have finished Shock Waves without you inspiring me to face this sober (and bringing me food).

Bobby, Christian and Mel, thank you.

I'd like to extend my compassion to all of those affected by the Bali attacks of 2002 and 2005, especially those who lost their lives, and their families, lovers and friends.

To all victims of terrorism, war and violence, I wish you peace. I hope that together we can find a way to celebrate the diversity of cultures in the world, and that we may learn from one another instead of fearing each other.

http://hanabethluke.tumblr.com
http://www.facebook.com/shock.waves.hanabeth

Contents

Foreword
by Tim Baker

THE IMAGE OF Hanabeth Luke the world knows best shows a young woman in shorts and a singlet helping a bloodied young man out of the flaming wreckage of the Sari Club. It appeared in newspapers and TV reports all over the world. The young man in the picture Tom Singer survived the blast but suffered horrific burns and died of a stroke soon after. It is a shocking image that captures the moment the Indonesia holiday island of Bali, and a generation of carefree travellers, lost their innocence.

Yet there is another less famous image of Hanabeth I find equally compelling, which depicts the steely resolve and quest for peace and understanding that such a nightmarish experience can inspire.

The young, tanned surfer girl from Cornwall, England, with her long sun-bleached hair, stands toe to toe with British Prime Minister Tony Blair. It is a scene from a televised forum in which Hanabeth and 17 other determined women with personal connections to the issue argued against the War on Terror.

They may not have swayed the British PM and the so-called "Coalition of the Willing" against their murderous invasion of Iraq. But Hanabeth's eloquent and impassioned plea voiced the concerns of millions unconvinced by arguments about "Weapons of Mass Destruction" and "pre-emptive strikes".

There is a quick and quiet exchange during the forum, when Hanabeth has pleaded with Blair to bring an end to the cycle of violence, which speaks volumes.

"There's nothing I can say to take away your pain," Blair offers sympathetically.

"I'm not asking you to take away my pain," Hanabeth replies softly.

It is this simple statement that I think captures what I find so admirable about Hanabeth's response to the Bali Bomb.

She has not shied away from the unimaginable pain of that terrible event and the overwhelming grief for her lost love. Instead, she has used them as a spur to live a full and meaningful life.

"When bad things happen to us it's easy to say it's happened for a reason," Hanabeth told me, as we worked on her manuscript. "It's not just that that reason comes out of the air and lands in your lap. You've got to make that reason and make your life better and make your own dreams come true. It's reminded me that there's limited time, helped me let go of my fears and go beyond my limits."

I first met Hanabeth through a mutual friend, who asked if I could help her get her memoir published to coincide with the 10th anniversary of the Bali Bomb. Initially, I was simply going to have a look at her manuscript, give her some feedback, try and put her in touch with some agents and publishers. Instead, I found myself being drawn into her story, contracting a small dose of her own remarkable determination to bring her memoir to the world.

This was mid-2012. The manuscript, though gripping and well-written, needed some work. A traditional publisher could never get it out by October, I advised. It might be worth considering self-publishing, a daunting and complex process for someone new to the publishing world.

Typically, Hanabeth threw herself into the task with boundless energy and courage, even as she worked on her PhD and continued her latest community work and inquiries into the Coal Seam Gas industry. When she went looking for an editor for her manuscript I found myself sticking my hand up almost against my better judgement, knowing full well the work involved, swept up in her infectious sense of mission.

In writing, re-writing, and reviewing her extraordinary life story, Hanabeth's shown an unflinching readiness to face all the most painful and uncomfortable issues that have arisen. She's matter-of-factly set to work to take on comments and suggestions, accepting sometimes brutal edits if convinced they served the story.

It seems fitting that a young, passionate surfer should have become the human face to this awful event, and spokesperson for a generation deeply cynical about the war-mongering of old men.

The global surfing community has formed deep ties with Indonesia and its people, traveling to its most remote corners, forming friendships, inter-marrying, forging the kind of cultural ties that the politicians only pay lip service to. By creating these real human bonds, travelling surfers and our gracious Indonesian hosts make lies of the narrow cultural stereotypes that seek to keep us fearful in homes, and in front of TVs.

Surfers were among the first to return to Bali after the bomb, and continue to visit cherished wave havens in remotes corners of the archipelago, despite natural disasters or civil unrest. Bali and its people have awakened many a western traveller to a different way of seeing the world – with their daily offerings of gratitude, a culture rich in ceremony, a gracious and resilient acceptance of what life throws at them.

Hanabeth is a classic modern product of this cross-cultural exchange, living out a seasonal migration between her little Cornish village, Bali and Australia since she was a baby. She is a true citizen of the world, for whom national borders and stereotypes mean little, whose natural habitat is the ocean that links all coasts.

I hope her candid and courageous story inspires many others to believe in the world they experience first-hand, rather than the one fed to them through media channels, to trust real human interactions over contrived sound bites.

Despite the terrible events of October 12, 2002, Hanabeth continues to find the beauty in every day, the good in people and inspiration and renewal in the ocean waves.

Introduction

The Swinging Pendulum

FROM AS FAR back as I can remember, my years were dominated by the force of a constant pendulum swing as I followed the summers from Cornwall to Australia, back and forth, back and forth, with a brief pause as each autumn turned to spring on the tropical island of Bali. The driving force of the pendulum's swing was my mother Maggi, one of the keenest surfers I know. She'd been following the surf around the globe since long before I was born. She helped to set up the Canadian West Coast Surfing Association back when surfing was just beginning, and lived on Malibu Beach when the '60s were in full swing. To support her wanderlust she'd become a successful entrepreneur, and since I can remember had been selling bright coloured Balinese wares at festivals, markets and in her own surf shops in both hemispheres. As she meticulously sketched out each year's clothing line to import for her shop, Magic Island, I remember the little cardboard cut-outs of the female figure, the stencil she used for her designs, multi-coloured and splattered with gold like a Gustav Klimt painting.

I'd sit at the desk next to her doing some sort of work, or quietly making my own designs, deliberately pencilling around the headless stencil with my clumsy childish hands. Sometimes the desk would be in St. Agnes, with the familiar pitter-patter of rain on the windowpane; the fresh green smells of the blooming summer flowers that lined the valley in which we lived. We would be wearing bright Hot Tuna sweatshirts over our summer dresses sitting on our swively chairs in the office. My father would be sat nearby working on his very large computer doing the books for his own business 'Magic Carpet Cleaners'.

In the heat of another summer in the same year, we would sit at the table together listening to a million multi-coloured lorikeets partying in the Norfolk Pines along an Australian beach, a voluminous and salubrious choir of tweeting like no other you will hear. I'd squeak as a large black spider walked across the wall above our heads. Mother would usually squash the misadventurous yet harmless huntsman with a big whack from a handy shoe (those were different times – we are happy to live in greater harmony with them these days).

What I remember most vividly is the blissful smell of the frangipani flowers behind our ears, and the taste of the mango, watermelon and papaya that would be placed on our bamboo table in Bali as Mum worked out her accounts and chose from the myriad of patterned, bold samples for her next summer range. The sticky, pungent smells around us mingled with distant melodic Balinese chatter. Combined with the incense drifting on the breeze these dreamy sensations made it very difficult to concentrate on my maths problems. In the mornings Mum and Dad went surfing, and sometimes they would take me with them. Other times I'd be left to play in the waves with a family of ten Balinese children.

No matter where we have travelled across the world, we always came back to our dear little village in Cornwall, St. Agnes, or Aggie. Three forested green valleys roll down into the sandy cove where most of my younger days were spent. Overlooking the village is the Beacon, a round-topped hill that gives a clear view along the tall cliffs and bays as far as the eye can see to the north and south, scattered with ancient fishing villages, and the ruins of the old mine engine houses. We always came back to our house in Castle Meadows, and we always stopped in first up at Goonbell where my beloved grandparents patiently awaited our return. My big brother Tommy and our big sister Mellie were around the village for my youngest years but, like most young folk around there, took off to work in warmer climes.

School was a more chilly affair. For most of my life I had been mainly in the company of adults as we travelled from place to place, learning guitar and chess from the travellers we crossed paths with. In Australia, I was the random blow-in from England and never stayed anywhere very long.

3

Back in Cornwall the children would regard this blonde, bronzed tiny girl with confusion as I turned up back in class with an Aussie accent mid-way through the spring term. I think the teachers themselves were not quite sure what to make of me. Most children found it easier to exclude me from their circles.

Then there was Lian Doble. Lian had had a three-week start on me when we met back in July 1980 when I was just two days old. Lian was the tallest girl in our class with short dark hair while I was the shortest, with a wild blonde mop. We were socially from opposite ends of the village. Her family built the most impressive residence in the village and ran a successful frozen food business, while my parents spent all our spare cash on surfboards and international flights. Lian was destined for a private education and god only knows where this wild child would end up.

The '80s were in full swing as our mothers enthusiastically pursued their careers, dressed in bright coloured dresses with shoulder pads (my mother's design). Jenny Doble was a psychologist who would later climb to the heights of her field. My grandmother, too, was a pioneer for women in her time, a tiny figure of steely resolve, not to be messed with. In today's society she would have been the general manager of the farm machinery producer where she worked. But in those days she could officially rise only to the position of 'secretary', although the consensus from many was that she ran the place for thirty years, pausing only briefly when her two sons were born, my father first and soon to follow, my uncle Geoffrey.

By the time I was born she had retired and enthusiastically threw herself into grandmotherhood. This was just as wonderful for our working mothers as they dropped us off at Gran and Granddad's place each morning. In one of the earliest pictures of Lian and I, we are sat on the couch with a mini-tea set. Lian's head is thrown back in laughter as I giggle mischievously, holding my cup up halfway with the red and yellow plastic teapot set down beside us. Little has changed between us over time.

We'd sit on the doorstep in the sunshine at my Gran's place eating the best Cornish pasties in the world. We threw the last piece of crust over our shoulders to the 'knockers' (the ghosts of the miners from Cornish folklore), so we could make a wish. Lian and I shared expansive and vivid imaginations, continually adventuring across the globe from within the confines of our own garden walls. One morning Gran opened her front door at the break of dawn to find two shivering six-year-olds out in the cold in their nighties, disappointed at not having found any fairies in the garden.

Lian faithfully awaited my return each spring, trying to help me to integrate with the friends she'd made while I was away. We were inseparable, going on bike-rides through the narrow bramble-lined footpaths, fingers and lips stained a dark purple from the bountiful blackberries that would cover the hedgerows in the autumn. Lian has an enormous family and many of our summer days were spent playing with her countless cousins, staying in 'The playroom' of 'the Croft', her big white home, together with twenty more of her young relatives.

But times started to change. I was picked up early from school one day to hear the news of my Grandfather's death. I remember so vividly the unfamiliar pain in my little heart and the tears that followed the loss of my dearest cheerful Granddad. The veggie garden lost its grandeur as my little Gran struggled to manage in the big house a mile away from the village centre.

My parents, who had always had a passionate relationship, were fighting more frequently and more viciously. The recession hit my mother's Magic Island hard, as she'd expanded the business at the worst possible time, losing everything and ending up in debt. At around the same time, she found out about 'the other woman' in Dad's life, so she threw his belongings out the window and down the stairs as fast as she could on Christmas Eve.

Dad came into school to see me when the new term started.

'Are you okay Hanabeth?'

'I'm fine Dad, don't worry about me,' I said, smiling.

'I do worry about you,' he said. 'I don't think you're as strong as you sometimes think you are.' As he left, we burst into tears.

I walked back out into the cold playground. Lian had moved to a 'prep' school a distant ten miles away, so I found myself entirely alone. The children, dressed in their grey winter uniforms, did not ask me to play. I watched the eddies in the wind pick up crisp packets and sweet wrappers with dead leaves and bits of dust, whirling them around and around in the frosty air as a cold chill moved up my spine that refused to go away. The pendulum had stopped swinging, so for the first time I was experiencing all four seasons in their proper order. The warmth of the Australian sun faded as my skin matched the pale colour of my classmates, and I was left to dream of tropical fruits and the scent of frangipani flowers. At home in Castle Meadows, Mum and I hid behind the couch from bailiffs banging on the door, there to take away our every possession, but we never let them in.

I drifted through the next few years in some sort of dream, staring out the window at the grey winter sky and the neglected plants in the school courtyard of mouldy concrete slabs. I threw myself into stories and artworks, doing the bare minimum I needed to do to make it through. Every report card said the same thing:

'If Hanabeth could only concentrate harder, or get more organised ...'

It was far from a bad life and, although the money was tight through the early '90s recession, somehow I still managed to travel a fair bit for a young lass, thanks to being the only child in a family of adults. Mum moved to Jersey to work for a few months and I flew over to the Channel Islands to visit her. Her dream had always been to ride in a red convertible, so for a treat she hired one in which we zoomed around the island with the Beach Boys blaring. I thought this was pretty cool (what was not so cool were the windscreen wipers that swished continually as neither Mum nor I could figure out how to turn them off).

My little Gran took me to climb the countless castle turrets and colourful spires of Bavaria in the dry summer heat, and my big sister Mellie flew me over to the Alps to visit her and learn to ski. Mum took me on shoestring trips to France. She freaked out in the claustrophobia of the crowded lift up the Eiffel Tower, so I carried on to the top by myself to see the seven bridges of the Seine stretched out below. She led me through the Musee d'Orsay where I saw Picasso's Guernica, hearing for the first time of the horrific realities of the world wars, and fell in love with the dreamy waterways of Monet and the rosy-cheeked country-folk brought to life by Renoir's light brush strokes.

In the summers Mum took me camping in France, driving six hours down the west coast, singing along with her old tapes of Tom Petty and the Eagles. Our campsite in Anglet was well known on the surfer/hippie trail, jumping with fun times and young people living out their summer break freely.

It was in the clear glassy waves of Anglet at one o'clock on August 1st, 1993, that Mum watched me paddle into my first green wave, hooting and clapping. I remember that wave so clearly and will never forget that feeling for all my life. From then on surfing was number one in my life, and started to shape my dreams, plans and actions.

I'd ask Mum: 'Am I as keen as Tommy was at my age?'

She'd pause for a moment, sweeping her long dark hair over her shoulder as she looked me in the eye:

'Not yet. Almost.'

Mum paddled out with me at my first point break on the Spanish border. I burst into tears when I discovered that the bottom was made of rocks. She tried to explain that was sort of the point of 'the point'. I eventually paddled out and proceeded to be a menace in the lineup, getting in everybody's way and wiping out on every wave. At another beach in Biarritz I got swept towards the rocks as the tide came in. On high tide there was no beach, only a seawall with waves crashing up against it. I paddled helplessly as each wave washed me further towards the black rocks. Mum caught a wave to me and I grabbed her leg-rope so she could tow me back to safety.

My brother Tommy had moved to the Gold Coast in Australia, and we hadn't seen him in over four years, so he paid for our trip to come and visit him at his half-built timber house on Mount Tamborine. At the arrivals lounge, we wheeled out our trolley from behind the frosted glass, clutching our surfboards. When we saw Tommy waiting for us, all three of us burst into tears. Four years is too long to not see your brother; your son (We also nearly got arrested for possession of a banana, narrowly escaping a $1,000 fine as the cute little kelpie had gotten fixated on the front pocket of my backpack).

We stopped in Bali on the way back, and *damn* I'd missed it. As the thick humid air hit us I felt so happy to be back among the rich sights, smells and sounds of the Island of the Gods. I felt at home walking down the dusty street amongst the hawkers who grabbed at my hair and called out:

'Plait your hair, wood carving! Afternoon price!'

'Tidak, terima kasih!' I said, stepping politely aside, and the men stood back in surprise and said, with a big smile:

9

'Speak Indonesian! Are you married?' To which I blushed and hurried on, much to their amusement. I *was* only twelve.

Weaving amongst the chaos and the crowds, frangipani flowers were everywhere, scattered on the ground and sitting behind the ears of the Balinese. Chained monkeys leapt out wearing little leather outfits; emaciated dogs wandered about, trying to scrounge a little pink rice from the offerings, nosing under burning incense sticks to be shoo-shooed off by stall holders. We jumped over the 'tourist traps', open holes in the pavement that led straight to the sewer below. I noticed stacks of colourful bracelets piled up on display and remembered the wristbands I'd made with some travellers at the campsite in Biarritz. I suggested to Mum that we could buy them cheaply here, so she bought a few bundles, and that was the beginning of her new business.

I was surprised to see how the craziness of Kuta (where Mum had long-since refused to go) was rather rapidly spreading up to the quiet end of town into Legian and beyond. I reminisced about when the streets were largely unpaved and most of the Balinese people would wear only sarongs, walking proudly down narrow lanes surrounded by lush green mango and coconut palms, scattered with dancing butterflies. As their sarongs morphed into jeans and t-shirts, I had wondered why the graceful Balinese wanted to dress like us?

In the early morning we paused with our boards on our heads to talk to the beach ladies who knew our names. They told us about all the changes, their usual smiles pausing into frowns for a moment, before they resumed their usual cheerful chatter as they tried to convince us to get a massage. What had been our 'Butterfly Lane' walk to the beach from Legian Inn had been turned into a rubbish tip, and we now had to walk the long way round the streets.

By the time we hit our teens, Lian was living and breathing for horses. Gran paid for me to have lessons, but every time I tried to go over a jump 'Honey,' my chosen pony, bucked me right on to her neck and I bounced along clinging onto her mane for dear life, to the great amusement of everybody else. I decided to stick to surfing.

In the spring of my fifteenth year I started to surf every day with my mate Nicola. Despite being a year younger, she'd always been much taller, her blonde hair in tight ringlets. Our mothers had surfed together since before we were born, and her dad 'Bunty' made 'Best Ever' surfboards and worked for my Dad sometimes. Nic lived a whistle away on the other side of a gravel carpark in a valley. She'd stand and whistle until I threw my window open.

'Coming surfing? Get your board!' she'd shout.

'Gimme five!' I'd call back sleepily. At least ten minutes later we'd each have a surfboard under our arm and a skateboard under our feet. We were pretty crap at checking the tide timetable (an essential habit if you're going to surf in Cornwall), so we'd often skate down bumpy roads for half an hour to find ourselves on a tiny rocky cove waiting for the tide to go out. Still, time was something we had plenty of, and it would not be long before the beach opened up and we'd be surfing the cold ocean together, looking back to shore at five long miles of yellow sand and the towering red and pink cliffs.

We surfed in our 5ml wetsuits, booties and gloves and sprinted up the beach in the winter hailstorms, sheltering under our boards. Sometimes in the summer waters we'd surf with our mothers in our bikinis.

Sitting together out the back, I asked Mum: 'Am I as keen as Tommy yet?'

'I think you might be,' she replied. I was beaming from ear to ear for a week.

My village is known to the locals as 'the Badlands', a party town with a reputation for a fierce local crew. They were mean to the girls too, throwing our clothes up onto the roof of the Surf Club, and once they hoisted Nicola's knickers up the flagpole. There was an old shelter that overlooked the beach and we would be curious about the sweet smell of hashish that wafted past us as we stood on the bench kicking off our wetsuits.

On my sixteenth birthday after a beach barbeque under a long, pink sunset I was given 16 'bumps,' which involves being grabbed by your limbs and thrown in the air. On the final one, I was thrown in the sea, but came back giggling to join a haze of dancing down at the smoky local pub, the 'Driftwood'. I'd finished secondary school and we were surfing, partying and getting into the pubs. We went to boat parties in fancy dress, and I discovered tequila (one of the loves of my life). Life was getting pretty fun but, like all magical eras, it didn't last long.

Mother and I were fighting regularly; it was a painful split as my independence grew. She is an amazing woman, but could be incredibly volatile and could *not* handle her alcohol. I ran away a couple of times to camp at the beach and surf unimpeded, living on a diet of bread and bananas. I worked for Dad to save money for the 'emigration', to Australia.

Mum and I left Nicola, Lian, Dad and Gran standing on the platform as we slowly chugged away from Truro station. Gran waved as she always did, until we were out of site, tears streaming down her face. Dad jogged alongside the train until he could keep up no more. I watched his moustache, his black curly hair and yellow t-shirt and jeans fall out of sight as he stopped at the end of the platform as our train rolled out of the station.

I pressed my face up against the cool oval window, feeling the hum of the engine right through my head, watching the clouds pass by and the blue shining surface of the Pacific Ocean below. We'd by-passed our tickets to Hawaii, Rare-tonga, Tahiti, Fiji and New Zealand following a fight over a remote control in LA. The reality of moving countries was already not as glamorous as I first thought.

We moved from the cold shores of Cornwall straight to the tropical paradise of Byron Bay, so Mum could surf her favourite wave, 'The Pass'. From a birds-eye perspective, the town nestles between a range of low green mountains covered with dense rainforest and a wide sandy bay of aqua blue overlooked by the lighthouse on Australia's most easterly point. Byron Bay itself holds a story of a remarkable transformation from a town dependent upon whaling, to a town which now relies on a tourist industry inspired by the perfectly peeling waves and (watching) the whales and dolphins which frequent the bay. The surrounding area, known as the 'Rainbow Region', hosted the Aquarius Festival of 1973 and was a pivotal point in the rise of the environmental and hippy movements, which still resonate strongly in the 'alternative' lifestyles enjoyed by the community today. I quickly realised that my adopted home was thick with crystal-wielding, rainbow wearing, guitar strumming, skateboarding local characters and travellers. No walk down the Byron main street was ever boring.

But riding barefoot with my electric blue surfboard in the racks of my electric blue bike under the electric blue Australian summer sky, I was miserable. I hadn't felt this lonely for a very long time. It was as if I had died and everybody that I had ever known and loved had been left behind, and I had gone on to heaven alone. Fuelled by the emotional pressure of our immigration, my mother's uncontrolled temper was clashing hard with my stubborn teenage angst. When Mother lost the plot, she smashed things up. I had brought so few possessions with me, and to see them smashed made me white with rage. As I pushed my mother out of my bedroom, grabbed her beloved underwater camera and smashed it on the floor, I did not like the person I was becoming.

The final straw came when she jumped on my blue surf-board. I packed my bags, grabbed my dinged-up board and jumped on my bike. She caught me, pulled me off and turned on the garden hose, soaking everything I owned. We screamed at each other on the front lawn as I struggled to get away before finally wrestling free, grabbing my board and sprinting up the hill as fast as I could with a trail of abuse following me.

Looking through all my soaked poetry books and dia-ries, I decided to never go back. When Dad came out a few months later, he stayed with Mum and never left. I supported myself through the rest of my schooling, finding myself in community housing for teenage school kids. A tall man with white hair was the social worker responsible for keeping an eye on me and the other two housemates, holding weekly meetings where we'd row ferociously. I was fortunate that he was incredibly philosophical and spiritual, an amazing guiding influence who helped me to recognise and break away from negative family patterns (Mum hated him).

A 'caretaker' called Beth lived downstairs to keep an eye on us. Beautiful, peaceful and inspiring, she introduced me to Dan and Nico. Nico was a tall marine biologist with short black hair who worked on the kayak tours and did whale surveys off the Cape. Dan was shorter with long curly brown hair and a love for multi-coloured clothing and music. They lived in the centre of Byron and I dropped by regularly on my skateboard. They shared their old wooden shack with Richie, another marine biologist who was taking a very long career break to enjoy the Byron lifestyle. We bounced out through the hills in Vanilla (Nico's high top Kombi van) to the bush raves, dancing until the sun came up over the multi-coloured hills. Nico, Dan and Richie became a huge guiding force in my life, teaching me a lot about fun and the beauty of all things quirky, and words like 'nefarious' and 'trippy,' as they took me on surfing adventures with their new eco-surf tours business, sleeping in a massive tipi. I trusted them implicitly and their acceptance of all my own insecurities and quirks went a long way to showing me the path to my own teenage self-acceptance.

I worked as a dish-pig on Sundays at a classic old Byron café, Ringos, where I met Stevie B. He was shorter than me with long dreadlocks, and also worked as a dish-pig. Stevie never stopped smiling, and picked me up at dawn to go surfing with his Canadian friend Jamie, dropping me off at school in his white Valiant. I spent a lot of time surfing and going on little surf trips with my Hawaiian girlfriend Kaale, and my Canadian girlfriend Tara.

It was lucky that I had such a robust group of older friends, because upstairs at my house was chaos. I lived with a succession of pretty lost young people, many who did not stay long. A lot of bongs were smoked up there, and much worse. There was plenty of alcohol drunk and some dark times; one angry young man on speed would run around the house smashing holes in the walls. Beth moved out from downstairs and Mia, a sixteen-year-old recovering anorexic moved in. We became close friends and I introduced her to Bob Dylan, Tom Petty and the Eagles. Then her best friend Rosie moved in. Mia was pretty conservative, but Rosie was a punk with bleached blonde hair, plenty of safety pins, DM boots and a great love for Hole and The Cure, which would continually blast through the wall to my room. She had a youthful innocence about her, yet was haunted by horrific childhood memories.

Rosie was a sixteen-year-old alcoholic who had already tried every drug she could get her hands on. She had a sweet yet reckless nature, hanging out with a small group of gothic girls who would walk together through Byron Bay dressed in black lace with pale white skin and dramatic eye makeup. I discovered the term 'self harm', hitch-hiking to the hospital to rescue both girls from the deep cuts they'd given themselves, or the overdose of pills they'd taken. It appeared my upbringing had been pretty good, really. A few days after my eighteenth birthday Mia burst through the front door, running up the stairs screaming Rosie's name. Rosie and all of her beautiful gothic friends had died in a house fire in Byron.

Needless to say, I was taking less and less of an interest in my studies, but it was my biology teacher who snapped me out of it. 'Hanabeth, you used to be so diligent. What has happened? You've only got a couple of months left which could make the difference to your whole life!' I saw the sincerity in his eyes and it clicked. What was I *doing*? I crammed for my exams with the Offspring on full volume. It paid off and I was offered a place at University. I took two years off to travel.

I arrived on Gran's doorstep to find the smallest, most elated woman in Cornwall with her arms open wide and tears in her eyes, pasties steaming on the table. I officially stayed at the Dobles but Nicola and I had somehow managed to rent a beach hut for one hundred and fifty pounds for the whole summer. Nicola worked at the Driftwood Spars, which was just two hundred metres up a steep hill from the high tide mark at Aggie Beach, known officially as Trevaunance Cove. I worked at Trevaunance Point Hotel as a dish-pig and chambermaid. It was a short but steep walk up Rocky Lane to the Dobles beautiful home, and we were pretty lazy, so we dragged a single bed down from the Driftwood, bought a cactus for decoration and moved in for the summer. Long story short, it was a summer of mayhem, hut parties and cold, clean waves literally on our doorstep.

The pendulum was back in swing, and once more the Cornish autumn turned to an Australian spring via the thick heat of Bali. Nicola came out to Australia for the new millennium. We travelled along the Australian coast and across the Indonesian islands, surfing the colourful reefs. We met two Americans out there called Tim and Bobby who became good friends and I'd see them many times more on that pendulum swing.

When we got back to Cornwall I worked behind the bar at the Driftwood, and up at Trevaunance Point Hotel on the cliff edge. I moved into Wiseacres, a dilapidated manor house in the centre of the village. The large window of my (almost) self-contained room peered down through the lush green valley that opened up into the blue waters of Trevaunance Cove. High cliffs peeled away to reveal headland after headland rolling into the distance.

While our little village could become stifling at times, life felt full of untold possibilities. Back when my innocent trust remained in tact, I never imagined that swinging pendulum was attached to a ticking clock.

Chapter 1

Touching Souls

I WAS WASHING TEAPOTS: big, expensive, china teapots rimmed with gold, dunking them in and out of the soapy water in the deep steel sink. They seemed so delicate and precious as I turned them over in my hands. With the slightest knock (as I had learned first hand), they could go from valuable to worthless in an instant.

The kitchen was a terrible place for a clumsy teenager to work. I burned and cut myself on a daily basis. The slightly tipsy owner of the Hotel took me aside one day.

'Hanabeth, I need to have a little chat with you,' he said, almost nervously, in his well-educated English brogue. 'We really love you working here with us, and you are an asset to the Hotel in many ways. It's just that...' My eyes went a little wide as I anticipated what he might possibly say next. '...If you continue to break the Wedgwood, I won't be able to afford to continue your employment!' I vowed there and then to be more careful in the handling of expensive crockery.

But this day I wasn't worried about my future employment so much as what I was doing back in my suffocating little Cornish village. The panes of the lead-crossed window looked straight out on a series of cliffs and headlands that melted away into the sea mist, if I cared to look. But as I scrubbed, I wasn't appreciating the beauty before me: I was fuming. I'd been back in Cornwall only days and already the village gossip had turned on me. As my breakfast shift finished, I walked into the dilapidated out-house to change out of my checkered work clothes and devise an escape plan to travel to France … or anywhere.

I grabbed my skateboard and rested it on my shoulder as I trudged up the steep hill towards the village. But I wasn't ready to face the village. Instead, I took a sharp left turn up a rocky footpath that cut over the hill rising between two valleys and led to the cove, flustered and confused. I'd inadvertently become mixed up in a village scandal simply by telling a friend too much information about her boyfriend's activities. Whoops. How was I to know it would end up in a witch-hunt for me? The little village that had known generations of my ancestors already felt choking. My little Cornish Gran seemed to be the only person keeping me here. I thought of her, tending to her beloved garden, watering the sweet smelling snapdragons that ran along the front of her little bungalow. Was she the only reason I'd come back?

Halfway up the hill, I paused at a wooden bench and sat down to look back down through the valley out to the expanse of shimmering ocean, through pink and yellow wildflowers dancing in the breeze. It was a magical, fresh, Cornish morning and the sky was unusually blue. Seagulls cried and swooped high above the cove. My mind whirred. I loved it here but I needed something to distract me from the trials of village life. I asked myself some important questions (because *that's how* you find out these things).

'So, what do I really want?' I thought to myself... 'What will make me happier here?' I sat for some time on the bench deep in thought (because I know you have to be careful of what you wish for!)

'Mmmm...' I answered to myself. 'I do want to be here, but if *only* a new person could come onto the scene to brighten up all this seriousness... Someone fun, slightly older and not involved in the bullshit of village politics. A traveller maybe... just someone to drive into town in their van and be my friend... an escape for me without my leaving... someone different and interesting... someone with an open mind... probably a surfer... Yes! And someone who can teach me guitar!' I smiled, speaking out loud to the whispering trees above me and the green salt waters below.

One thing I do know is that if we articulate clearly enough what we want in this life, and it comes from our heart, just sometimes that call is answered.

After a late evening surf, I rushed up from Aggie Beach, keen to get home to a hot shower. I'd stayed out long after the lifeguards had left, losing any hope of a lift up the long road winding towards the village. In fact, I'd been the last in the water. The sun had long-since slipped behind the tall cliffs that surrounded the cove, casting a cool shadow over the rocks and the sand. I carried my surfboard under one arm and my skateboard under the other (it'd made it much easier getting *down* to the beach). As usual, I was wearing just a T-shirt and shorts with bare feet. My long brown hair was tied in pigtails that each dripped a steady stream of cold water onto my clothes. I shivered and my cheeks grew rosy as I puffed up the short sharp hill between the beach and the pub.

My surf buddy Nicola had already run up to the pub to start work a couple of hours before, so I thought I'd pop in on my way past. The sun still illuminated the bottom of the valley where the pub sat nestled amongst the yellow gorse and mauve heather.

The Driftwood is a big old stone building with a great granite fireplace, old pews and heavy wooden tables, with pint glasses and flagons hung up along the curved bar. The thick black beams that lined the smoke-stained ceiling were built from the driftwood of wrecked ships. Perhaps we all do something like this with our lives, try and salvage something solid and comforting from the misfortunes that befall us. How many souls had been lost amidst those shattered timbers at sea, yet how many others had found laughter and companionship within their shelter?

I propped my boards up outside between a flower box and an old pew. As my eyes adjusted to the darkness, I recognised the landlady behind the bar.

'Hi Jill, have you seen Nic?' I asked.

Jill answered in her soft Cornish accent: 'Sorry love, don't know where she is. We're pretty quiet so I sent her home. Oh, hang on! There was a few of them hanging out in some grey Kombi in the car park. Go 'ave a look!' She pointed out the door.

A grey Kombi van? I wandered out to see the van in question in a corner of the car park. It was parked under a tree with the side door open and a light on inside. 'Interesting,' I thought as I peeked inside and said a shy, 'hello.' I got a few back. I knew everybody except the good-looking man in the driver's seat. He had short, black, spiky hair and a big smile with straight white teeth. He sat on the high-backed chair with a guitar resting on his lap. The van was obviously his home and had a simple setup – a long side bench and a double bed covered with a blue quilt. A long surfboard lay on the bench and several local girls were perched on the bed, including Nic.

'Hello, I'm Marc,' he said cheerfully, holding up a big tanned hand.

'Hi, I'm Hanabeth. Nice to meet you,' I replied with a smile, holding out my small tanned hand.

'Come in!' he said as our hands shook. I climbed in and sat on the floor leaning against the bed with one leg hanging out of the door. Through the car stereo, Jeff Buckley crooned one of my favourite tunes.

'Where did you get that from?' I asked him. 'I haven't heard Jeff Buckley in England before.'

'An Australian friend gave it to me,' he said, leaning over the seat towards me. Australia, a topic I love, touched on straight away. It was his dream to travel there, he said. The other girls' expressions grew bored as we chatted excitedly. I tried to change the topic to a more inclusive one:

'Hmm ... It's getting a bit cold.'

'Here, wear this jumper!' he offered, tossing me something big blue and woolly with a fish design on it. I put it on gratefully. *Lilac Wine* started to play through the speakers.

'Oh! I love this song!' I said, smiling at Marc.

'It's my favourite!' he replied excitedly, smiling back at me. I noticed a small, carved, wooden fish hung around his neck, resting upon his grey top. When I asked about it, he told me that he'd carved it himself.

As we chatted, I learned that Marc had just moved to the village but had grown up not so far away, and he was a little older than us. He told us he'd been surfing for a couple of years, and Nic and I shared some stories from our recent travels in Australia and Indonesia. Marc apologised for his board taking up too much room in the van, so I suggested he tie it up against the window with bungees. I became aware that an uncomfortable silence was spreading through the rest of the van. I knew what the local lasses could be like with new men in the village, so I withdrew from the conversation and concentrated on rolling a spliff, inhaling the sweet hash perfume deeply before passing it around.

We went into the pub for a bit, drinking cider under the cosy low ceiling. After the pub shut Marc gave a few crew a lift up the hill, dropping me off last. We waved a cheerful goodbye, but by this time I had already told myself: '*Don't even think about it!*' I did not want to join any competition for the hottest new blood in town or make any more enemies.

The next night as I hiked up from the beach they were all sitting in the van again. I had left my block of hash in there so I popped by briefly to grab it – that was all. Marc hadn't noticed it and so I found it right where I'd left it on the floor. I didn't stay for long, but several things happened in that short while. I noticed he'd fixed up his board with bungees already, so there was a lot more room. I sat on the floor again with my back to the front seat. Marc was sat on the bed strumming his guitar, and he was rather good. He glanced at me and smiled, catching my eye. Something moved through me like a shudder or a finger down my spine, an unfamiliar but strangely pleasant sensation. It is a moment frozen forever in my mind, such a simple image of the smile he flashed me. His dark chocolate eyes, white teeth and cute tanned face sent my heart thumping. Looking back, I now know I had seen a flash of what was to come, and some of that chemistry must have leaked through my shield. I thought to myself how my perfect man would surf and play guitar … but I rapidly pushed such ideas away. I said my goodbyes and drifted on up the road, leaving the local girls to it. I was trying to get my head straight by simplifying my life, which involved keeping clear of boys.

Living in a small village, I bumped into Marc nearly every day and each time we seemed to isolate ourselves in conversation. Predictably, he had started 'seeing' one of the prettiest girls from the original group, who sat between us glaring into the distance when we chatted, hanging on each others' words. Feeling guilty, I would tear myself away and wander off. It must have been obvious that I felt excited every time I saw him.

I remember the date we got together very clearly. It was Nicola's birthday, July 12, just six days after my own 20th birthday. I sat in the Driftwood waiting for Nic to arrive to celebrate: she was due at 8 o'clock. Although the ale was great, as time went on I started to get a little annoyed. Glancing at the old brass clock on the wall I saw it was nine-thirty, and I had a good idea I was being let down for the umpteenth time by my dear old pain in the arse friend. As my eyes flicked back across the bar I noticed Marc walk in from the lounge bar and sit down with what looked like a glass of coke.

I didn't pay much attention as I was busy drifting off in thought, musing on some red-haired boy I'd started to date. I'd just found out that as far as my friend, flatmate and work-mate Charlotte was concerned, so was she! He was probably congratulating himself on having two women on the go (without realising that we lived *and* worked together).

Marc sat across the bar on his own. I looked over and our eyes met. His face lit up as he waved, so finally I plucked up the courage to cross the room. He greeted me with a smile and we soon began empathising about our ill-fated relationships. His romance with the pretty local girl had recently ended due to her kissing other men in front of him.

'Hmm ... perhaps she has other ideas about commitment!' I giggled.

'Yeah, not for me,' he replied, shaking his head. I told him I was waiting there for Nicola.

'That's not a way for a friend to behave,' he said.

'Oh, it's a long, long story. She's one of my oldest friends; she's great fun. I mean I just travelled Indo with her, but she can be a royal pain in the arse too!'

'Do you like JD?' Marc asked suddenly.

'What?'

'You *know*, Jack Daniels Whisky!' He was grinning widely, his eyebrows raised.

'No. Can't stand whisky.' His face fell.

'Do you like Tequila?' I asked with a cheeky smile.

'No.' We must have both looked a bit disappointed.

'Do you like Sambucca?' he asked.

'Yes!'

'Right,' he said decisively. 'On Friday night, let's get together and drink a bottle of Sambucca and damn the rest of them!' Sounded good to me. All of a sudden I realised the situation: He single; me free; him wanting to spend time with me, just me. My heart did a little leap. I suddenly realised that I really quite liked this guy. There was a magnetism between us that was proving difficult to ignore. Marc dropped me home to Wiseacres, and I asked him in for a smoke and a cup of tea. As I closed the curtains I looked down through the valley to notice the ocean reflecting a glowing, pink sky.

We sat on my king-sized bed and chatted away merrily listening to Jeff Buckley. As *Lilac Wine* began to play, he leaned across and playfully took my hand. Like electricity, I felt every millimetre of contact between our fingers as my gaze met his. With our eyes locked together, he pushed my hand against his until we were palm to palm, my tiny left hand pressed against the long, slender fingers of his right. As I felt the roughness of his skin, the gentleness of his touch, my heart began to skip and a hundred butter-flies were let loose fluttering through my chest. Suddenly we were leaning towards each other with our eyes still locked. His left hand reached up to stroke my hair with the softest touch. I watched his intense dark eyes come so close as his lips met mine with the most beautiful kiss I had ever known.

What was it that made us click? I'm not sure, but we sat up all night lost deep in conversation, kisses and laughter. Everything we talked about we felt exactly the same way: how we looked at life, not taking things too seriously, con-stantly making fun out of every situation, truly seizing the day. He wanted a girl who loved life and smiled her way through the day, a girl who was up for any random and crazy scheme. Marc had married young, and had worked as a mechanic in Cornwall since he was a teenager. Now he longed to travel and explore the world, and I was a traveller, ready for a companion to explore it with. I loved his silly jokes and boundless energy, his joy for life and determina-tion to make the most of it. We had made the transition from me to us in a few hours. Whatever happened, we could see this was going to be a whole lot of fun. By daybreak, we were deeply in love.

When Friday night came, we drank Sambucca down at Aggie beach as planned. We sat on the rocks and watched amber waves rolling up the shore. I studied the high forehead and spiky black hair of Marc's profile as he looked up to watch the sun drop below the headland. We had a wild time drunkenly stumbling up the jumble of steep footpaths back to Wiseacres in the dark. When I ran ahead, Marc called out in mock fear:

'Don't leave me here! I don't speak Cornish!!' Laughing, I stepped out of the darkness and passed back the bottle of aniseed-flavoured sweetness. We stopped on the wishing bench to look back down through the valley to the swirling moonlit sea, leaning towards each other in the darkness.

On the first day we spent together we took off for a surf and picnic a few miles up the coast. We'd parked at the end of a rough sandy track that wound its way back towards civilisation. The long straight stretch of open beach was lined with a network of sand dunes that gave the place its name, Perran Sands, and the long trek down to the beach kept it relatively uncrowded.

We felt the tough seagrass and the soft sand between our toes as we started down the slope, warm under our bare feet. I remember watching Marc's milk-chocolate back moving in front of me, his left arm sticking out a bit to counteract the weight of his self-made longboard. His blue boardshorts rested on his hips before stopping half-way down his long gangly legs. Marc ran ahead and as he bounced down the hill he disappeared behind a dune. He was waiting for me just out of sight, grinning as I rounded the corner. The dunes dropped away drastically in front of us and the shimmering summer ocean stretched out as far as the eye could see. I fell against his chest as I kissed him, throwing my free arm around his neck. Our boards bumped together.

'Oooh sorry!' I said grinning.

'Ah, you'll be in trouble next time!' he said with a flash of those teeth. He grabbed my hand and led me down the last steep pathway between the dunes, sliding onto the beach.

The surf was small but clean and fun with a strong off-shore breeze. Marc and I paddled out together and sat out the back chatting happily between waves.

'You could do with a longboard!' said Marc, as he watched me struggle to gain speed on my six-foot stick.

'No thanks!' I laughed. 'Those are too much work getting past the waves, let alone trying to turn the things.'

'Ahh, one day you'll see the light!' he chuckled as he swung his board around and caught a wave that peeled all the way into the beach. I was wondering if this gorgeous man would really come back to Australia with me. My return flight was only a few months away. So many talked of travel, but it never happened. It's so easy to dream, but to turn dreams into reality?

When our surfing was done, we walked together jumping over the big ripples on the sand, splashing in the puddles.

The tide was low and there were miles and miles of exposed beach, beyond which we could see the cliffs and headlands down the coast towards Aggie. We found a secluded spot halfway up the dunes for our picnic, laid out the food on my upturned board, making a feast out of our meagre provisions – banana, tuna, corn, salad and fresh bread rolls. I had a disposable camera with me and Marc held it at arm's length with one hand to snap our first photo together.

As the sun eventually dropped towards the ocean it was time to trudge back up the steep dune, stopping by the Kombi to admire the sinking sun sparkling on the ocean. Marc leaned down to kiss me, our calf muscles aching as salty lips and sandy hands entwined. The sky mellowed into a golden pastel sunset as we drove up and down the green valleys back to St. Agnes.

Falling in love is a crazy thing. Even my menial tasks in the old hotel couldn't wipe the smile off my face. I would be cleaning the old floral rooms or helping the chef in the tiny cluttered kitchen, making smoked salmon roses and happily plunging my arms into the soapy water, scrubbing the cast iron pots and pans with a massive grin on my face (carefully handling the teapots). All I could think of as I pulled the sheets off the beds or stopped to stare out of the window was being back in Marc's arms.

My daydream drifted back to that morning when the sunlight spilled through my window to outline his body resting on my white embroidered sheets. The rest of the world blurred to insignificance as I floated in my happy dream, thinking of the warmth you only feel from soft glowing skin on skin, lips melting in love and passion. I snapped back to the present to hear the footsteps of the elderly housekeeper Ena plodding down the corridor. As the door creaked open she lectured me on my lack of cleanliness in the last room. I suppressed my giggles at her serious expression and Cockney accent. I could not get annoyed – my mind was already dancing straight back into Marc's arms.

Marc had taken me for a drive along the coastal roads towards Lands End. His longboard and my little yellow six-foot shortboard rocked side by side in the back as the kombi leaned round the corners, chugging our way out of the village. We swung right at the big three-lane roundabout at Chiverton Cross and onto the dual-carriageway of the A30, heading south. Before long, we turned off into a narrow coastal lane, the Kombi squeezing between high hedges, brambles scratching at the paintwork. Marc knew all the back roads, cutting through farms and down rocky unpaved lanes. The hidden roads wrapped round hills and through valleys thick with green trees and scattered with weathered stone barns and cottages. They curved through gorgeous little coves splattered with coloured summer flowers that brightened up the windowsills of old whitewashed Cornish pubs. We drove past the ancient church of St. Just on the windy hillcrest of the coastal moor. Heavy monuments lined the road alongside big granite outcrops bare amongst the spiky yellow gorse and pink heather.

One of my favourite surfing spots in Cornwall is Gwenvor. It was the cove where I experienced my first taste of bigger waves back when I was 15 – taking off on an overhead close-out set, looking up at what seemed like a massive wall of green with adrenalin pumping through my veins. We turned into the car park at the top of the big cliff and bumped our way into a parking spot overlooking the isolated cove – a bit of a local secret spot. There was a white granite headland to the south, and a rocky outcrop to the northern end separating Gwenvor from Sennen at the base of the towering cliffs. The water was clear and blue with small yet perfect waves.

'Small and perfectly formed. Just like you!' Marc said. I rolled my eyes, grinning.

As I opened the car door the wind grabbed it and tried to wrestle it from my hands. We huddled together, peering over the cliff.

'Wanna go surfing?' he asked.

'Not really, it's pretty small and very windy. Not too inviting! Shall we go for a walk down to the beach?'

'Yeah! Let's go!' said Marc.

We chased each other down the steep path to the coarse yellow sand. There were lots of rock pools further up the beach, and large expanses of rounded boulders. We sat on a rock, and I looked up and down the beach. A couple of kids were playing in the sand with their dad; a middle-aged couple stood at the base of the cliff path, and one guy was sitting on his longboard in the water waiting hopefully for a wave as he got blown slowly out to sea. An elderly lady walked her dog up the cliff path. They were all at the other end of the beach, and the rocky area on which we sat looked down on them all.

I gave Marc a cheeky look, and with an expression of pleasant surprise he raised his eyebrows at me. I smiled and both our eyes cast down between two large rocks in a sort of sheltered gulley. Our eyes moved from the gulley to each other. We giggled and climbed down the rock, holding hands and keeping one eye on each other and one eye on the rest of the people on the beach. As we leaned together my hand rested on the nape of his neck, my fingers gently touching the cord that held his fish pendant. My fingers ran round the right side of his neck, following the cord to the front, down to where the wooden fish rested inside his blue t-shirt. I pulled it out, examining it ... and gave him a sudden kiss. He drew back gently as he looked me in the eye.

'Hanabeth, I want to come with you to Australia,' he said. As my heart soared, he curled his arm gently around my waist and pulled me close as his soft lips answered mine ...

'So 'Anabeth, you will go back and clean the toilet in Wheal Prudence won't you?' A harsh Cockney voice cut in on my daydream.

'Oh!' I replied, for I was back in the hotel, and Ena was standing a metre from me, giving me a serious look and expecting an answer.

'Oh yes, no problem Ena,' I said convincingly.

'Hrmph.' And she was gone, shaking her head as she waddled back down the narrow pink floral corridor clutching her air freshener and a feather duster. 'Girls these days,' I think I heard her mutter.

I wandered into the bathroom, and set to cleaning the bath, allowing myself to drift back to my daydream.

I met Marc's parents Carole and Ray after we had been together not much more than a week. He talked about them all the time, even when he was seeing them every day.

'So, you're the girl making our boy so happy!' cried Ray as he climbed out of their Toyota van. He was as dark as Marc, though not as tall, with a lovely warm face and welcoming expression. Ray had driven Carole to drop off a big bag of clean clothes for Marc.

'Pheweee, the pong!' she exclaimed, as she held her nose up and chuckled at the new filthy sack presented. It was a brief hello that first time but their utter cheerfulness struck me. Marc had told me that they loved to walk the endless Cornish cliff paths so were both in good shape for their age. Ray was nearly seventy, tall and slim, and Carole was in her mid-sixties, her curls cut into a neat grey bob.

Not long after that, I went to their house for the first time. I was a little nervous as I knew Marc was 'the one' for me. Marc held my hand as I teetered down their short bitumen driveway in my platform heels and mini-skirt. The house was so quaint, a proper cosy old Cornish cottage, with big stones in the walls and white painted wooden windowsills. Window boxes spilled flowers bursting with colour alongside the front porch. 'Come in!' was the excited call from within, and as the door opened I fell immediately into the warm arms of not one, but two big hugs.

'Welcome to the family!' cried Carole. I must admit to being a little overwhelmed. I was ushered in to tea, biscuits and chattering conversation, lots of questions, smiling, and interested nods. I quickly realised that they were the perfect 'normal' parents I had always dreamed of. Ray was rock solid, handy and dependable; Carole was always cheerful, pottering around the kitchen or the garden, ready to cook up an omelette at any given moment. I was delighted with them as I guess they were with me. I was part of a new family.

In St. Agnes, I took Marc around to meet my dear little Gran and experience Cornwall's (hence the world's) best Cornish Pasties. She loved having someone else to feed, and eating was Marc's forte: He ate *three* pasties, and not small ones either. They got on like a house on fire. Gran was most impressed as she shovelled custard on to his stewed apple and rhubarb. She looked at me over Marc's shoulder and winked. I beamed back. Gran's approval meant the world to me.

One of the first things I told Marc was that an air ticket was never going to be found in the bottom of a glass of JD. He wasn't earning enough to save, he'd said. When I told him what I earned and how much I managed to save, he went quiet. Before I knew it, he had announced that he had cleared his debts, and soon he was saving money. After a couple of months he sold his Kombi and had bought his ticket out Australia for that following Autumn. We were both working hard, but work was just fun, and problems washed off me like water off a duck's back. My life was paradise and no one on this earth could take that feeling from me.

One day Marc and I went out surfing at Porthtowan, a short low-tide walk along the sand from Chapel Porth. The waves were a bit bigger this day so I was excited as I paddled out in the rip. I noticed Marc looked nervous. As we got past the breaking waves, I sat up on my board but Marc paddled an extra 50 metres out to sea. I shrugged my shoulders as I turned and paddled for a left-hander, dropping down the face and racing through the section to ride up over the white-water and paddle out again. The other surfers sat in a scattered pack just beyond the impact zone, but Marc was even further towards the horizon! I paddled out to him.

'Hey, send me a postcard when you get to Ireland,' I said laughing. He didn't laugh, so eventually I paddled over to him. 'Are you okay?'

' Yeah.' He didn't look convinced. He looked even more nervous.

'What's wrong Marc?' I asked.

'Well, I can't really swim so well,' he replied angrily.

'What! You're kidding right?'

'No.'

'How have you managed to surf this long?' I asked in disbelief.

'I just don't lose my board, and I haven't surfed waves this big.'

'Oh.' I paused. 'Well, you won't catch anything except the freak sets if you stay out here! Why not go further in and catch a smaller one. I'll keep an eye on the horizon for you.'

Marc shrugged in agreement and paddled in a bit, taking off on a wave that was not really lining up properly. I saw the splash as he wiped-out on the take-off and I heard him swear loudly. He popped up a few seconds later with a look of panic. Another wave broke on his head before he was able to clamber back onto his board and paddle back out past me again, fear on his face as he sat up and looked warily out to sea.

'What happened?' I asked.

'My head went under the water!' I stared at him in amazement (it's a pretty common occurrence when you surf).

'I've got a funny nose,' he continued, not looking directly at me. 'What?' I refrained from giggling.

'When I go under water, water rushes up my nose. I hate having my head underwater!' He was almost angry as I fought back a smile.

'It's only water!' I said.

'Easy to say,' he replied. I was surprised. Marc was seriously scared. I swallowed and adjusted my facial expression accordingly.

'Okay, have you ever tried holding your nose as you go under? You've just got to relax down there. Don't fight it.'

'I dunno, I just hate having my head under-water. I had a scary experience when I was a kid. I waded out and found myself out of my depth and couldn't get back to shore. I've always been afraid ever since.'

'Didn't your parents teach you to swim?'

'They're not really beach people,' he responded, shrugging his shoulders. We both leaned back on our boards for balance as a line of swell rose up under us and passed us by. I watched JK, a friend from Aggie with white-blonde hair, paddle like hell to catch it and disappear behind the white-water. I could see Marc watching longingly.

'I wish I'd learnt to surf before, but I only started when I was 26.' I nodded in acknowledgement. JK had been surfing since he was six years old, like most of the people I knew from here, born into the heart of the surfing scene. I could understand Marc's frustration, but I didn't know what I could say to help him. He did eventually catch another wave and went in to watch me surfing from the sand. I realised that I would have to be a little selective on the waves I dragged him out in from now on.

Marc was still technically married, although they'd separated several years before. Marc said she was the first woman to take an interest in him, but had come from a troubled family. At that time he'd been a different man: shy and skinny with pale skin and long black hair tied back in a ponytail. His passion back then was racing cars and doing up his little vintage Mini. On the day of their wedding, her father stole the ornate silver knife, so when the time came to cut the cake the knife was somehow discovered down the trouser-leg of the father of the bride. Marc told me she'd been very insecure and incredibly possessive over the course of their six-year marriage, and had threatened him with violence many times. She hadn't liked it when he'd decided to learn to surf and about two weeks after he started, she threatened him with a kitchen-knife. Within an hour he had packed his car with his surfboard, guitar, a few books and clothes and drove away, never to return. By the time I met Marc he was confident, tanned and strong, a free and happy man with a bright future.

The days of our first Cornish summer started with the fresh sun peeking through the curtains in my big room at Wiseacres as the birds chirped their morning song. I can still hear Nick Drake crooning on the CD player as we awoke locked in each other's arms and our eyes flickered open to find the other's gaze inches away.

'Never felt magic crazy as this … Never held emotion in the palm of my hand … felt sweet breezes in the top of a tree … but now you're here, brighten my northern sky. It's been a long time that I'm waiting …' Together we played between the white sheets, laughing and loving.

Nick Drake crooned: 'Would you love me through the winter, would you love me till I'm dead?'

Chapter 2

Exploring Cornwall

IN CORNWALL, LOCAL knowledge is everything. Marc had already spent ten years driving around exploring the valleys and the coastline in the years before he surfed – and since, from a surfer's perspective. Although I'd never driven myself, Mum would always take me on day trips visiting all the surf shops around the coast, selling her Balinese jewellery and trinkets to shops hidden away in coves and valleys all over Cornwall.

When I was a kid, sometimes Dad would pick me up from school. There was usually a mystery tour involved with the journey home and I never knew quite where we would end up. Once, we were driving along the straight Roman road home to Aggie, and without warning Dad took a sharp right onto a narrow lane cut between high walls of green. My response was to release a teenage groan of impatience – I wanted to get home to surf and hang out at the beach.

Into the valley we plunged, past an old stone cottage. 'Your great-great grandfather built that!' Dad announced excitedly. We drove through a broken gateway onto a bumpy lane where overgrown gorse and branches scraped against the sides of the van, the strip of grass in the middle of the lane as overgrown and neglected as the high hedges on either side. We pulled up at an old barn and tiny farmhouse where Dad started telling me about our ancestors who lived there two or three hundred years ago. As a teenager I didn't appreciate the impromptu history lessons.

A few years older, and with Marc at the wheel beside me, it was so much fun to seek out these places among the riddle of winding Cornish lanes. After three and a half years living in a country where a building from the '70s was considered old, I now appreciated my deep Cornish roots. Marc loved the adventures, as fascinated by everything about me as I was with him. I loved the chance to get out of my St Agnes bubble and see some other places. It was the second summer I'd come home since I'd moved out to Australia with my mother, but the only wheels I'd had were the rubber wheels of my skateboard. Marc drove me to all the places he loved to surf, like Gwenvor and Crantock, Sennen and Constantine. He took me to ride long rolling waves at low-tide beaches on dry, sunny Cornish days and I led him to more powerful waves that broke in shallow water. We'd trot down the cold sand in the rain clutching our boards under our arms. After a run back over the dunes to the car park we ripped off our wetsuits in the rain and climbed into the Kombi to get warm, sitting on the bed cleaning the sand from between our toes while hot chocolate bubbled on the little stove.

Only weeks before I met Marc, Nic and I had been travelling Indonesia together, two tanned and scruffy Cornish girls with wild blonde hair and lots of surfboards. Slightly nervous about travelling across the islands alone, we'd teamed up with tall skinny Bobby and wide-grinned Timbo who were staying in the room next to us at Cempaka, our cheap losman in Kuta. They were travelling with a couple of other friends who accompanied us on the infamous 'Two Day Bus' to Sumbawa, hurtling along dark roads at terrifying speeds, stopping for noodle soup and a pee at curious roadside huts. The journey was intersected by two very rusty ferry rides crowded with curious Indonesians. This was true budget travel, and had sounded slightly less terrifying than the rattling flights that took you straight to the surf camp on Sumbawa, if you were lucky. The guys had guided us safely on our journey and showed us where to stay and where to paddle out at the powerful reef breaks. Between Timbo and I, we'd managed to convince eight people to paddle one kilomometre across the dark lagoon for a full-moon surf out at Lakey Peak.

Timbo was accident prone to the extreme, and between surfs in Sumbawa had told us of way too many hideous accidents and injuries that he'd been subject to over recent years. If you could catch him not grinning, Timbo would probably look a bit scary out in the surf with his big frame and missing front teeth (left next to a mangled bicycle on a roadside somewhere). But as soon as he commenced his regular giggles the true Timbo shone through: a party animal extraordinaire who liked a good joke and found most things funny. I had a habit of travelling with a small bear that I called Nipper, whose job it was to take care of me on the road. After Timbo took such good care of us on our trip (and after hearing his stories), I gave Nipper to Timbo so that he would be looked after on his future adventures. They'd become great friends, yet it was impossible to know then how much I would desperately need them one day. Thankfully, that day was far in the future and many good times were to come first.

After we'd left Bali, Bobby had kept on travelling through South-East Asia, but Timbo had come back to Cornwall for the summer. Like myself, Timbo followed the pendulum swing of the Australian/Cornish summers, spending his British summers living in a little village in North Cornwall called St. Merryn. They were living less than an hour away, so we went up to visit them for a weekend. It was great to see Timbo, with his booming infectious laugh, and Marc and Timbo instantly liked each other. He had a large pile of colourful Balinese boardies so Marc bought a red and blue pair. 'Why are men's clothes usually so dull?' he asked, tossing his old grey shorts aside.

On the Saturday night in St. Merryn, we went out to a big rave amongst the dunes. Unfortunately, before a lot of dancing could take place I'd drunk too much and felt sick. Marc sat with me on a quiet dune and too care of me, stroking my hair and making sympathetic noises.

'Please, I really need some water,' I said, looking pleadingly up at Marc. With no water available at the party, we left early in the morning and became completely lost down the dark winding lanes on the two-hour trek back to our campsite. Marc held my hand all the way as he guided my unsteady footing. When we woke up in Timbo's caravan some hours later, a pile of bedding on the floor began to move, from which appeared a smile as wide as Timbo's amongst a wild head of curly brown hair.

'Hello!' she grinned through hungover eyes, as Timbo's head also appeared. That was how we met Polly.

Over the weekends, Marc's friends Simon and John regularly came round to hang out at Wiseacres. Charlotte lived upstairs and would often come down to join us (happily our friendship had survived the redheaded boy). My old friends Matt and Laurs often came too. We sat around in the summer evenings exchanging dreams, stories and village gossip, making plans for the winter. Like most young folk in the village, none of us planned to stick around when the autumn leaves fell, whether we left off on a coach bound for the snow covered Alps, drove down the European coast chasing warmer waves or flew off to Bali and Australia.

Parties are as prevalent as pasties over the Cornish summer, and the locals cram as much mayhem as possible into the limited warmer days. There were famous quarry parties which people came to from all around the county, held in a deep old quarry owned by one of the numerous members of Lian's family. Timbo and Polly came down for a visit with some other friends from St. Merryn, when a quarry party was rumoured to be on. We walked carefully down a stony cliff path with a glimmer of the late sunset on the horizon, hearing a faint beat somewhere in the distance. Matt led the way holding Laurs' hand and Simon, John and Charlotte followed closely behind Marc and I. Suddenly the gorse in front of us opened up to reveal the quarry, as the music pumped and coloured lights scanned and flashed across the crowd and lit up the quarry walls. Fire twirlers performed on a natural stage, throwing their fire sticks high in the air, deftly catching them and spinning straight into another swirling pattern. As we slipped into the centre of the seething throng of dancers, we could feel the beat coming up through our feet as if from the earth itself.

'Let's climb up!' said Laurs with a grin, so Charlotte and I followed her up the rock face to stand on our own stony platforms. As we danced, we faced back across the quarry, pointing our pink flashing wands over the sea of grooving young folk. Matt jumped on the DJ decks and mixed up some tunes and the crowd just kept getting bigger and wilder as we danced the night away.

While many of us were on ecstasy or cocaine, Marc would stand firm that he was high enough on life already. We were still dancing when the first pale rays of the sun crept over the western hills, so we danced our way out of the quarry to where we could see down from the cliffs onto the expanse of rippling ocean. Old ruined mine buildings towered above us, surrounded by tired and/or high friends in the on-going celebration of youth, madness and summer. A friend of ours led us to a Secret Garden that he had created, hidden amongst the low heath on the cliff top, featuring a lily pond and a herb garden of rosemary, mint and oregano. He'd carefully lugged up beautiful stones to rim the flowerbeds, and a pretty little wooden bench sat amongst the white pebbles of the path. We snuck a look out to see colourful escapees from the Ball wandering along the cliff-path in the distance, feeling rather smug in our hidden oasis.

Summer is so short-lived in Cornwall that not one ray of sun is left unworshipped, not one opportunity for a good party passed by. Every little town has its own carnival celebration, when the whole village dons fancy-dress garb and joins any one of a procession of floats connected to a particular club or pub. Aggies' was wilder than most. There were huge water-fights when everybody hid an arsenal of water-bombs and water-pistols underneath the floats that moved slowly around the one-way roads.

Kids and their parents held up water-pistols from their second storey windows to shoot us as we passed by. The Aggie Hotel let the fire hose loose on the Driftwood float while dropping cans of beer down a long tube from a small balcony to their own float as it passed by. Between smartly dressed marching bands and fairy-queens, pissed-up villagers danced around in choreographed displays dressed as sea-life, Mexicans and Pirates. Half embarrassed, I waved sheepishly at Gran who did a double-take as I passed her by sporting a super-soaker, dressed as a gypsy with a red bandana and a big fake piercing hanging out of my nose, running to catch up with a big old hippy bus. Marc stood next to her, taking in the whole scene as it passed by: it was not quite the same in *his* village!

As the evenings started to draw in and rainy days replaced the sunshine, we spent a lot of time eating steamed puddings and watching movies, snuggled beneath my big quilt at Wiseacres. It was a different sort of paradise, but it was all ours. From partying lots, Marc and I had simmered down to maybe popping down to the Driftwood for a drink on the weekend. All we really wanted was to come back to our refuge and cosy low lights of my room in the dilapidated mansion, formulating our plans to move out to Australia together.

'So, come on, tell me about Byron Bay!' said Marc with an interested smile.

'Okay, so, as you know I've lived there since we emigrated when I was sixteen … It's like no other place you've ever been, nothing you've ever seen. No walk down the main street is ever the same twice. The people are as diverse as the landscape. There are lots of hippies, latte drinkers and backpackers, but you also get clowns, wizards in top hats, techno-colour dresses and rainbow flags flying, especially at the markets. You'll find all sorts of funny folk, like fairies who will paint your face for a dollar, fortune tellers, artists and candle makers, all selling their wares as the musicians play for all to dance along to. Or you can sit and eat all sorts of delicious food like you've never even imagined. There are lots of activists in Byron Bay too, people who want to help make the world a better place, people who really care … Lots of environmentalists, and *boy* that environment is worth protecting!'

'What does it look like? Paint me a picture!' asked Marc excitedly.

'Well … at the foot of lush green rolling mountains, there lies a wide bay rimmed with yellow sand. The shallow, sparkling waters are rich with fish, dolphins and whales. If you're lucky they jump right out of the water! At the end of the Bay, a white lighthouse is perched on a green headland, looking down over the town and out to the expanse of ocean where perfect waves peel steadily through and … and … it is a rare place where people even love …'

'Love what?' asked Marc, leaning towards me in anticipation.

'They even love … LONGBOARDERS!' I grinned widely.

'Ha, ha, ha,' Marc laughed happily.

The summer was racing so fast to the end that it was nearly time for the SAS Ball. Ahh … The Ball! It's hard to explain to one who has never had the pleasure, but I'll try. The SAS Ball is a fundraiser party of gigantic proportions held by Surfers Against Sewage (SAS), which was founded by Aggie people and still bases itself in the village. SAS got together because so many of us were getting mouth-ulcers and sick stomachs from turds floating past the line-up. They'd managed to sort out the Aggie sewage system first, and for the benefit of surfers everywhere were now busy taking on the rest of the country. Despite the important cause, most members joined up so they could come to 'The Ball'. The SAS Ball was always on the first Friday of September, looked forward to by many as the event of the year. Members of SAS come from all over Europe to attend the massive labyrinth of big white marquees placed high on the Cornish cliffs between the valleys of St Agnes and Chapel Porth. The Ball had a different wacky theme each year and this year it was the Rio Carnivale Ball. Most local girls had been picking out tiny colourful frilly outfits since they sobered up from the last Ball, I am sure.

The night of the Ball blurs in my memory as a succession of coloured lights and music, surrounded by fabrics of gold and silver, flowers, frills, feathers and g-string bikinis. Normally, I would be off adventuring, bumping into different friends for a dance, before disappearing off on another random adventure. This time was different. I felt no need to run about or leave Marc's side as we danced and adventured together until the glowing dawn lit our winding, skipping trot back to the village along the cliffs.

But, we didn't go to bed yet. I'd decided that it was a tradition to have a wetsuit-free, ceremonial surf down at Aggie before sleep could be permitted. The swell was clean and fun, and we loved the novelty of having the waves to ourselves, myself in a bikini and Marc in his boardies. An early surf in Aggie usually takes place at about 9am, but we were in the water by seven, surfing until the cold finally sent us running up the cobbled shore. We just about crawled up the hill to fall into bed. Of all days, my dear Gran decided to pop around at about 9am to drop off some cake for us.

'Gran!' I declared in surprise. As I opened the door to her neat grey curls, I heard the thump of Marc landing on the floor behind the bed. I tried hard not to giggle.

'Marc's car's outside,' observed Gran. Not wanting to burst her old fashioned bubble, I told her he had stayed at a friend's place nearby. How stupid did I think she was? You'd know every trick in the book after eighty years… *wouldn't* you?

Right after the ball, Laurs, Matt and Nic took off with a few other mates on a road trip to France and Spain, so Marc and I stayed in and ate more puddings, or headed off on our weekend surf missions. We shared a love of music – there was always music playing in Marc's little Corolla and we sang along together to his tapes as we drove and David Gray urged us to sail away now…

It was *our* song, because soon we would be off. We were planning to go farther afield that winter. We'd both done enough drinking, partying and talking gibberish, and now were busy saving money for our new life together. Marc had sold the grey Kombi to pay for his flight, and we kept his Australian ticket in a place that we could see it when we woke up at Wiseacres. He was so excited to finally be going to the place he'd dreamed of for so long.

On one of our surf missions, we pulled up at the beach but the tide was too high so Marc pulled out his guitar. I loved watching his long fingers slide up and down the neck of the guitar as he strummed out a song for me. He sat in the car leaning slightly out of the open door, his thick brow knotted in concentration. As he relaxed into the tune he started singing. I noticed he was getting louder, better, more confident. And somehow I discovered that I could remember the words to most of the songs he played. When he'd first started playing for me he had whispered the lyrics.

'Open up!' I had cried, 'I bet you have a wicked voice!'

The main gift I gave Marc was to help him build his confidence in the waves. He had already started to teach me to drive in his little Corolla and had given me the chance to start singing, but he also taught me little practical things about how to live, while I showed him how to let loose and fly. He taught me how to love unconditionally ... Well, maybe we learned that one together. Over time, Marc gave me something I had never truly felt I had: a rock to depend on. Someone who knew me so fully, loved me and would always stand by me. When I crumbled and the bouncy façade was showing cracks, his arms would be there, along with soothing tones to calm my storm.

When big things went wrong, like an accident, injury or loss of money, when Marc had smoke coming out of his ears it would be me who kept my head. I would be philosophical and Zen, talking about life's rollercoaster ride. We'll make it through, I'd say simply, as he envisaged the world's end.

Marc took me out to a '70s night in Newquay to meet his best mate, Dave 'the Rave'. Marc thought the world of Dave and always had something good to say about him. They had me in hoots of laughter as they coordinated their moves to YMCA in floral shirts and crazy flares on the flashing tiles of the dance floor. I hadn't seen him quite in this light before.

Marc found my phone calls from my mother amusing at first. There were two categories of calls I would receive; the excited calls bursting with information about what she was doing, how the business was going, and the surf she had at Wategos Beach that morning. I would pass the phone on to Marc and they'd have a nice chat for a while. All was sweet. Then the other type of call would come and my face would fall as I heard the first word.

'Yes, Mum.' I'd listen to her whinge about Dad or Tommy for maybe ten seconds before holding the phone away from my ear, look at Marc, raise my eyebrows and shrug, resignedly. Marc's eyebrows lowered as he saw my expression, but he would laugh, and at the time, so would I.

The nights drew short and cold as we spent the end of summer surfing frigid, messy waves and eating hot Cornish Pasties, puddings and custard at my Gran's little house. I'd soon be flying to Bali for a stop-over, tending to some business for my mum, before traveling on to Australia, where Marc would join me. The time apart would be a torment but Marc needed to save more money before we'd be together again.

I'd booked a train ticket to London a week before my flight to Bali. So I did not stress as we lay in bed for a last cuddle before Marc drove me to the station. Our landlady Margaret tapped on the door, speaking urgently:

'Have you seen the news, Hanabeth? I think you'd better turn the tele on!'

And there it was: disaster! We had somehow completely slept through a huge storm that had caused major floods, washing a large portion of the railway tracks away. There was no way of getting to the airport in time, so I quickly arranged another flight for five days' time.

I spent this strange time in limbo at Marc's parents' cottage in Carnon Downs, about a 20-minute drive inland from St. Agnes. Instead of going back to the village and explaining to everyone why I was still there, and having to say my goodbyes all over again, I chose to enjoy their wonderful hospitality and hibernate at the cute little cottage. They put a blow up mattress down on the floor of Ray's little music room for Marc and I to sleep on. The weather that week stands out in my memory because it did not stop raining once, and it was freezing! I was housebound during the days while Marc worked at Imperial Motors saving his last few pennies. The nights drew in so early there was no chance of a surf after he got back, but who wanted to go outside in that weather? It was a lovely comfort having Carole looking after me, feeding me omelettes and endless cups of tea. I watched an unusual amount of TV and read trashy magazines. As wonderful as it was when Marc bounced through the door after work each day, I was relieved when it was finally time to leave Cornwall.

Chapter 3

Love in Paradise

I LANDED AT DENPASSAR Airport clutching a small piece of green, folded card. Marc had given it to me as a parting gift, and inside it I kept a beautiful picture of him I'd taken myself. He sat in the open window of an old engine house on the cliff at Chapel Porth; his dark eyes looked out towards the open sea. He had written in winding patterns all over the green card, so I had to turn it around, upside-down and sideways to read the most beautiful words that had ever been written for me.

I'd been in Bali with Nic just months before so I guess I was pretty blasé about this trip, which was something like my 24th visit to the Island of the Gods. I was there to do a little bit of business for Mum and the trip went by in a blur. I found it hard to sleep without Marc by my side, and in the daytime I walked along the dusty streets in a dream, wishing only that Marc could be there to share the overload to the senses that was Bali. Happily Timbo and Polly had also stopped in Bali en route back out to Australia, and Bobby was basically still there.

Leaving the chaos of Kuta behind, Bobby took me out to Canggu on the back of his bike, weaving in and out of the constant flow of trucks and motorbikes. Timbo and Polly zoomed along behind us with Polly's wild hair flying in the wind and her big grin sticking out from under her helmet. We wound our way through the lush rice paddies to find waves peeling across the reef. I put on my reef-boots and paddled out in perfect waves, pledging to myself that one day I would surf these waves with Marc.

Before I knew it I was back in Australia staying at my parent's place, where at least I could call from the land-line and hear Marc's voice. He was leaving the next day and I spoke to him excitedly about what awaited him in Byron Bay. Under his instruction I'd bought a longboard so he could surf upon his arrival. To avoid the trouble of the train-lines being closed, Marc had brought a plane ticket straight to Gatwick from Cornwall.

As I woke up the next day I felt excited to know that he'd be in the air by now, but I was surprised to hear Mum call out to me:

'Hanabeth, er, Marc's on the phone.' Confused, I grabbed the receiver to hear Marc's depressed voice.

'You won't believe it, I missed my flight!' he told me sadly.

'What! How?' My heart sank as he explained that once again the Cornish weather had intervened, grounding all the planes at Newquay Airport, so he'd missed his connecting flight. His brother Steve would later show us footage of the happy Marc, so excited to board his flight until the moment he heard the news. He literally fell to his knees in frustration upon the grey tiles of the airport floor, ticket in hand.

'It can't be possible!' I said. Not to happen to *both* of us. But it had, of course. Thankfully it wasn't too difficult for him to change his ticket for a few days later, but those few days still felt like a thousand years for both of us. Marc booked the early flight, giving himself a twelve hour stopover at Gatwick, just to make sure that there was *no* way that he could miss *this* one.

I still didn't have my driver's license, so Mum and Dad drove me to Brisbane airport to pick Marc up. We arrived early and I stood staring at the frosted glass as trolley-rolling travellers appeared, waiting impatiently as Mum and Dad stood behind me. They were keen to find out what all the fuss was about.

After a small eternity, Marc appeared. In reality, I did not have to wait so long before the flash of his white teeth and his black spiky hair came around the corner. He was the first off his flight! He strode over and his arms enclosed around me. Finally I was holding him so tight.

'That was *too* long, I don't want to be away from you ever again,' he whispered into my ear. As I felt his kiss on my cheek, I glowed with happiness.

By the time Marc had reached Byron Bay, there was no time to waste. We had to see it *all*! I'd registered 'Mousy', a rusty Lite-Ace van so we had a set of wheels that could fit in his huge new 9'6" surfboard. I took him straight down to my favourite beach, winding along a bumpy dirt track, bouncing down a steep, overgrown path to step off onto white sand. I stood laughing as Marc danced around, loving the feel of the hot, squeaky sand between his toes. A large pelican was poised on the water's edge, watching this strange human. We had the whole cove to ourselves as we paddled out. Marc caught one perfect peeling right-hander in to the shore, but as he came off the wave he cried out in pain:

'Ahh! What's blue and hurts?' he said, half panicking. I started to paddle over and saw a familiar thread of blue tentacle on his arm.

'Oh dear, that's bad luck. This is a blue bottle,' I said, pointing to a little shimmering bubble that floated on the surface nearby.

'Will it kill me?' asked Marc. 'It bloody hurts!'

'No, it wont kill you,' I smiled. 'Catch another wave and the pain will go away.' Marc's eyebrows knitted as he remained unconvinced. 'You didn't tell me about *these*!' he muttered grumpily.

After spending Christmas on the beach with my family, we quickly found a shack to rent at a small suburb to the south of Byron Bay. We moved our meagre possessions in for a summer of sunshine and clear crystal water. I cooked pasties and invited Dan and Nico, Kaale, Richie and Tara to bring all of their partners, so they could meet my wonderful Marc. My friends were stoked to meet Marc, and he was stoked to meet them. He was especially inspired by Dan's multicoloured clothing. When we'd finished our pasties, we all threw the last bit of crust over our shoulders and made a wish. The boys picked up their guitars and the music flowed for the rest of the evening.

Marc was still pretty nervous of the ocean so I tried to help him gain confidence in the water. I preferred to surf Tallows where the waves were bigger and more powerful, but Marc wanted to surf Wategos where the waves were smaller and perfect for longboarding. Often we'd compromise with a surf at Broken Head just down the coast, which was protected from the bigger swells by a rocky headland, but there were also more powerful waves further down the beach, so we were both happy.

It was at Broken Head I tried to help Marc overcome his fear of going underwater. We stood facing each other in waist-deep water as I spoke to him slowly and calmly.

'So, the aim is to get a handful of sand, okay? Reach down so your head is just under the surface, and bring me some sand, right?' I looked at Marc as he nodded and then disappeared under the water, coming up holding out his hand, which was filled with white sand. I took a little from his big palm, thanking him.

'How's that?' I asked smiling.

'Yup, fine,' he answered, smiling back.

'Okay, so we're going to go a bit deeper now, alright?' Marc nodded and followed my instructions as we proceeded out deeper and deeper in the crystal clear water. Within an hour I had taught Marc to take his feet off the bottom and spin a full cycle forwards and backwards underwater, holding his nose between his thumb and forefinger. He swum a bit, and he really wasn't too bad. He just lacked confidence. I gave him a couple of basic tips and we swam along the shore together. We drifted further down the beach where the waves were bigger and I showed him all the ways I knew for jumping in, under and over the waves. I taught him to relax, to not fight the wipe-out and instead to wait and let the wave pass by, to go with the turbulence rather than fighting it.

Just north of Byron Bay, sandwiched between a network of canals and a long strip of a white sandy beach is the Gold Coast. 'Surfers Paradise' consists of glitzy nightclubs filled with big-breasted blondes and buff gym junkies, flashing neon lights and skyscrapers resting right on the shore of the Pacific Ocean, casting great shadows over the sand each afternoon. To most people I know in Byron Bay, the Gold Coast, or 'the Goldie' is the embodiment of development hell. It was finally time to start my studies up there.

Looking back, it was surprisingly one of the most blissful periods for Marc and I. As uni began, we moved from our sticky summer unit in Byron to my big brother Tom's cool house up on a mountain in the hinterland behind the Goldie. We drove up the winding mountain road that led to the house that Tommy built on Paradise Drive, Eagle Heights, on Mount Tambourine. I don't think I'll ever beat that address, nor the beauty of that house. It was set on stilts standing out from a sharp slope right on the ridge top. Strong, dark haired Tommy had been a carpenter and builder for many years, and had been working on the house for some time with Darrell, a close friend and bricklayer. Beautiful stonewalls laid with shells led us down the steps to the front door to be greeted enthusiastically by Beachie, Tommy's yellow staffie. The timber door with coloured glass panels gave way to high white ceilings, floors of polished timber and walls painted a deep reddish pink.

Tom gave us the big bedroom on the top floor. The morning sun flooded mercilessly into the windows as it rose over the ocean. Our view stretched as far as Brisbane to the north, down past the hills of green, softly rolling out to the coastal plain and into the suburbia of the Gold Coast. The strip of high rises lining the coast looked like anthills in the distance. Our time up on the mountain was peaceful, except for the family of kookaburras who liked to wake us early with their laughing and pattering on the roof. We drank Tom's fresh coffee together on the veranda before rushing off into the bustle of our days. I gulped down pints of rainwater straight from the tank – I've never tasted water so sweet.

Uni started and Marc packed me up a lunch and set me off out the front door with a gentle kiss. Marc quickly found work with Tom's mechanic, working halfway down the mountain at a place called Mobile Spanners. I now had my learner's license, so on our weekend surf missions down to the coast I drove under Marc's instruction, and he told me I was nearly ready to take my test.

For all the magic of living up with Tommy in his beautiful house, we were simply too far from the waves. At best we were a forty-minute drive to the surf, so after a couple of months of heavy tropical storms and cool summer evenings on the deck, we were on the move again. Up at Tommy's house one night, Marc pulled out a map of the Gold Coast and said:

'Right. Where do we want to live?' We located the uni, we located the beach, and the closest place we could be to both was where Marc's finger landed on the map.

'There: not too close to Surfers, but the whole place is close to the beach and not too far from Mobile Spanners. What's it called?'

'Main Beach,' said Tom darkly. Although he understood the surf was calling us, he didn't want us to leave.

'Okay then,' I said. 'Let's live there!'

Tommy shook his head in exasperation. 'Good luck,' he said. We didn't know it at the time, but we found ourselves living on one of the most desirable (in other words yuppie) streets on the coast, notorious for its strip of expensive cafes and restaurants. As usual, we had no idea and totally fell into the spot.

We went into Main Beach Real Estate and asked if they had any cheap places to rent. We had been continually told it would be impossible to get a place there in our price range, so we moved into the first and only place we saw. It was a small block of four flats that looked just about ready to fall down, but in the right spot on the map. Besides, we had a garden, were close to the beach and it was only a ten-minute drive or a short bus ride to uni.

We settled in quickly, rising before dawn to skate down the road with our boards under our arms. We were usually the first in the water when the air was still and the water flowed like quicksilver. It seemed that wherever we chose to surf, the next surfers to come down would paddle out right where we were. Once a few crew had joined us we'd paddle fifty metres to an empty peak just as good as the first. When they eventually followed us over, we'd paddle back to the original peak. There were plenty of waves for everyone and each day there seemed to be perfect swells rolling in with that orange-yellow sun as she crept up over the horizon.

Despite being in amongst the tall anthills, in many ways we loved where we lived, right in the heart of the city. A couple of the towers were really quite beautiful and we dreamed about what it would be like to live on the top floor, right there on the ocean's edge. We sat together out the back, waiting for perfect glassy lines to peak up right where we were. Marc took on the right-handers while I rode the left-handers to the shore. Often we'd pull off our waves to face each other along the shore's edge and laugh, before paddling back out to catch another one. Marc was gaining more confidence in the bigger surf. He certainly didn't have any trouble putting his head under water any more. In fact, it was hard to keep him out of the water.

Marc drove halfway up the mountain each day, loving his job and becoming close friends with his boss Peter. I finally passed my driving test and we drove the Lite-Ace up to visit Peter, his Indonesian wife Eppi and their little daughter Emily. I was enjoying re-engaging my brain at uni, joining the free gym and starting to make a few new friends.

They'd often come to visit us at Main Beach, sitting in our little enclosed garden with sweet smelling frangipani flowers all around while galahs and lorikeets played in our tiny oasis. Beyond our gates towered the forest of skyscrapers. We discovered we were living on what was known as 'The Strip', and every hoon on the Gold Coast would scream past at 2 am in their jumped-up metal cans to pull doughnuts not far from our door. Every place has its imperfections.

Despite the quirks of our suburb, we were settling in. We applied for Marc's Australian residency as a de-facto couple, so we took a whole lot of photos of ourselves and got a joint bank account. Marc bought a vintage electric guitar and amp and we sang together in the evenings over a few drinks. Marc started creating beautiful furniture out of camphor laurel logs that Peter had given him. We wandered around home-ware stores buying rugs, crockery, cushion covers and a beautiful shiny saucepan set, all made to last. I bought a second-hand sewing machine and started making colourful clothes for us both.

Under Marc's working visa, there was a rule that you couldn't work at any one place for more than three months, so just as everything was going perfectly, he had to leave dear Peter at Mobile Spanners. Tommy helped Marc out with work in Brisbane but he had to be up and gone by 5am, so we lost our mornings at the beach. It didn't help that we had an insomniac neighbour living above us who liked to move furniture around all night long. Our other neighbours were party animals who came home at two or three in the morning and partied until the sun came up. The screeching sounds of the doughnut-spinning hoons seemed to get louder. It was starting to feel like time to move on. Finally, the whole building received notification that we had to leave, as the place was going to be knocked down.

Living in the city had started to take a toll, I was craving some green space and Marc felt the same way. It finally occurred to me, I never had checked out Southern Cross University (SCU) in Lismore, just inland from Byron Bay.

We walked across the lawns of SCU with a lady who was chatting away to us about campus facilities and details of the course. I wasn't really giving her my full attention, as I already knew that I would be coming here. As we'd opened the van doors, I had felt instantly at home. I loved the greenness; the contented looks on the students we passed by; the friendliness of our guide. She pointed out koalas in the eucalypts and showed us the remnant rainforest. As we stood quietly by the lake right in the middle of the campus I wondered why I had not come here before. Marc and I exchanged an almost imperceptible nod, and a smile.

'The new semester's already started. When can I make the move?' I asked.

'As soon as you can,' the lady replied, smiling warmly.

We drove the Lite-Ace back through the rolling hills, exploring the winding lanes.

'So, where do you think we should live?' asked Marc.

'Dunno, I'd like to be outside of Byron maybe,' I said thoughtfully, watching the pattering rain on our windscreen run into rivulets. 'It's a bit too crazy in town. I'd love to be up in the green … but not too far from the ocean.'

'Its stunning here,' replied Marc finally, as we drove down through a lush valley, past a tiny little shop nestled on the hillside. Instinctively, Marc turned in to the Tintenbar store and pulled up outside. The old wooden floorboards creaked under our feet as we shared a jelly 'rainbow python', and wandered over to take a look at the notice board. Marc pointed to a tiny note scribbled on a ripped piece of lined paper.

SELF CONTAINED ACCOMODATION, BROOKLET.

'*What's a Brooklet?*' whispered Marc. I shrugged my shoulders.

'What's a Brooklet?' we asked the shopkeeper.

'It's a place,' he replied, pointing out the shop door in a northerly direction. 'Ten K's that way.'

We drove through some of the greenest, quaintest hillsides I'd seen in Australia, so much like our home of rolling fields and forests back in Cornwall. The weather was wet, and the roads damp. Marc drove our little white van cautiously round the winding bends, peering through the foggy windscreen as we splashed through the puddles.

'It's pretty basic,' said our landlord-to-be as he glanced around the shed that sat amongst an orchard of macadamia trees. He was about forty, bald, and very tall, dressed in heavy boots and (very) short, blue workman's shorts. We looked around at the open space and the bare cement floor, with two thin ply walls thrown up in one corner to make a bathroom, and two more sheets of ply in another corner to make a bedroom. There were no doors. The thin aluminium outer walls were a simple army green colour, broken up by dirty metal beams and supports full of spider's webs. The ply walls were painted with purple bug-eyed cartoon fish and in the kitchen fake tiles had been painted on. Two tiny windows made for dingy lighting, and the only insulation was on the ceiling high above, spilling open with yellow foam in the far corner.

'Would you mind us doing it up a bit?' I asked.

'I don't care what you do with it, as long as I can still get my tractor in here if I want to some day,' he replied. We exchanged an excited glance. Already we could see the palace we would create here.

Chapter 4

Trouble in Paradise

WE DROVE A vanload of stuff down from Main Beach to Brooklet and Marc stayed with me on the first night. As I walked into my first lecture at SCU, Marc was already three hours north, finishing his last week of work in Brisbane. On my first night alone in the shed, the bush outside was full of howling sounds that I wouldn't have noticed if I were wrapped safely in Marc's arms. The shed itself seemed alive, shifting and creaking in the wind. There was no ceiling on the walls of the 'bedroom', and I lay in bed with my eyes wide open, stiff from the cold and from fright. The ceiling reflected the grey moonlight that spilled in through the bedroom window, casting moving shadows on the vast roof. There were mice too, picking their way through the boxes scattered over the shed floor. The door rattled, the shed creaked. Axe murderers and rapists tapped on the walls trying to find a way in … It was a night of no sleep.

Five days was a long time for us to be apart, but it got much better once Marc was back (I would not be cold for the rest of the winter!). I lay cosy in his arms, listening to him breathing, feeling his body give off heat like a radiator. The murderers on the roof revealed themselves to be possums and dancing birds, awaking us to a clear blue sky with the glory of their song. The tapping on the walls turned out to be the branches of macadamia trees. The great fig tree beside the nut shed was rich with life: the whip birds, kerrawangs, swallows and colourful parrots sang and chirped all day long.

Marc quickly found a job at 'Byron Car Sales', so we busied ourselves into settling in. It was mid-winter, so first we found some patches of carpets to cover the bare cement floor. We didn't have any money, but together we were pretty resourceful and never felt as if we lacked anything. Our landlord gave us some hardboard with which we lined the thin walls. Marc noticed a big pile of bamboo by the roadside a couple of K's down the track. It was easy to make friends with the farmer, who didn't mind us taking as much bamboo as we wanted, and from then on he waved when we drove past each day. There was a small section of the shed in the corner next to the bedroom that we decided would be our living room. First we partitioned it off and made a bamboo ceiling with curtains along the front, so it felt like a den from the Nights of Arabia. We made the den cosy and warm first, the bamboo and creamy hemp cloth creating a beautiful atmosphere. Marc put up a shelf for our stereo and the music started to play. I filled in one wall in a mosaic pattern using short lengths of wood, which also provided insulation. Two narrow beds in one corner made for our couch, and we covered them in brightly coloured retro fabric. We adorned an old half-wooden TV with furry blue and pink fabric, taking great care to glue the fur neatly around the buttons. We hung up the saucepans; covered the walls with paintings I'd collected or painted over the years, and set down our quirky assemblage of ornaments; the orange lava lamp, Marc's old surfboard fins and a clear plastic retro phone lit up by a tube of purple light. We named our home The Nutshed.

Once we had it all together, we sat huddled in our 'den' in the evening. Marc strummed his guitar and when I recognised the chords I started to sing: 'Don't you know they're talking about a revolution. It sounds like a whisper…' Marc sang along with me. Both of our voices were getting louder, stronger, more confident, echoing off the walls of the Nutshed. We slept in our basic bedroom under a quilt of shimmering blue. Our little window faced east and we could see the sun rise through the rows of macadamia trees running down the hill towards the coast. I'd wake to find Marc with his face pressed against the window, watching the clouds:

'It's offshore, I think. Let's go surfing!' he'd say, poking my shoulder through the covers. I'd groan but eventually rolled over until I fell out of bed onto the cold floor, somehow taking a further quarter hour to get from the floor and into Mousy. We'd often stop off at a little stall on the way to pick up some bananas, dropping $2 into the honesty box outside the farm.

The short drive down the hillside to Broken Head sometimes revealed a choppy ocean and deserted beach with waves at ankle snapping height. Disappointed, we'd plunge in anyway for a swim and bodysurf before heading off. Marc had no hesitation with the water now. His trademark move was to sprint at top speed into the water before hurling himself at a wave. It took me so long to get into my bikini, wax my board and get down to the sand that Marc would usually be the first out in the surf.

One morning we'd pulled up in the sandy car park and Marc had already run down to check the waves, and I paused to hear the news on the radio.

'Two planes have flown into the World Trade Centre in New York,' said the newsreader, with uncertainty in her voice. Marc came bounding up to the van.

'The waves are perfect,' he said, then seeing my confused eyes he asked: 'What's up Hb?' He touched my hand.

'Not sure,' I replied with a furrowed brow. 'I don't think it can be real, but I just heard some crazy news. They say there's been a terrorist attack in New York. It sounds more like a movie.'

'Really? Nah, surely not? We can find out later. Let's go surfing babe.'

We headed for the beach to ride waves that had travelled vast distances across the ocean, blissfully unaware of larger ripples already set in motion.

It takes a special state of mind to start a garden, to sew seeds that you intend to nourish and care for until you can reap the fruits of your labours. Plunging my hands into the earth felt symbolic, for a gypsy girl like me to be settling down, digging my own roots into the land for a while. While Marc was at work, I spent two days with a shovel creating a pretty and neat-edged vegetable garden. Marc came home grubby and tired from a hard day under oily cars to find garden beds ready to be planted, and a tired girlfriend sitting on the front step with a shovel, satisfied grin and two cold drinks waiting.

Mum, who was now an avid gardener, gave us all types of seeds so we planted rows of tomatoes, capsicum, peas, carrots and cucumbers. Soon the garden was flourishing, and when summer came it would provide us with delicious meals of potatoes, spinach, tomatoes and the biggest juiciest cucumbers I've ever tasted.

Marc's job, welding up and preparing the used cars meant that we always had a second car, which was pretty handy. I was now in full swing at uni and had already made some new friends, but my life really revolved around Marc. A couple of guys from my classes lived close by and we started to car-pool for company and to save fuel. Some days I left uni late. My Monday lecture didn't finish 'til six, and sometimes I had to wait for a lift from my new friends Lee or Andy. Sometimes I was just really keen and working on an assignment, so I drove home in the dark. I knew that when I got home, there would be a light on at the Nutshed, and the door would open to a big smile and a warm hug.

Marc made it clear very early on in our relationship that he was scared of losing me to my studies, as he felt he'd already lost his last two girlfriends that way.

'They just changed. Nothing else was important any more, just studying,' he said. 'You'll see! You can't help it, you'll just get wrapped up in it and forget about me!'

'Honestly Marc, I could only dream of ever being lost in my studies!' I said, laughing. 'I think you know me better than that!'

Nevertheless, Marc had a great plan that I should go to uni 9 to 5 each day, treating it like a full time job. That way, when I came home, the time was ours. I kept that up for quite a while, and how I would look forward to coming home to Marc, our simple meals, eating chocolate mousse from plastic tubs in front of the furry TV. We started doing yoga with my Canadian girlfriend Tara twice a week, and sometimes Marc stayed to play guitar with her husband. Sometimes, if there was time before sunset, we took our skateboards to the lane at the top of our driveway and practiced walking up and down the boards on the smooth slope, riding switch-foot.

For the first time ever, Gran finally came out for a visit, and she travelled with Marc's folks Carole and Ray. We constructed a second bedroom so they could stay with us in the Nutshed. It was so special for our families to meet each other, and to experience the rich, beautiful lands in which we lived together. We shared some magic times up on Mount Tamborine, staying at Tommy's place. Marc's passion for guitar had come from his father Ray, and this they shared with Tommy, so they spent the evenings playing together for hours. I'd sing along with Mum, Carole, Gran and Beachie sitting beside us.

One morning just before dawn, I awoke to find Marc crying. Shocked, I moved over to hold him, putting my hand gently on his cheek:

'Babe! What's the matter?' I whispered. In the weak grey light he turned to look me as he choked back loud sobs.

'You died, babe. I was left without you,' he said mournfully. 'It was the saddest dream I have ever had.' Marc looked so, *so* sad, sadder than I had ever seen. 'Don't ever get yourself killed...' he said.

I pulled him as close as I could, whispering: 'I'm right here Marc, and that's where I'm gonna stay. It was just a bad dream... nothing but a bad dream.'

One thing I have come to realise is that no matter how much in love two people are, there will inevitably be challenges. From the beginning, I had always valued the time we spent apart as essential in maintaining our own selves within our close relationship. When we first met in Cornwall I explained to Marc that we needed to spend two evenings apart each week. At first he found this hard to understand, yet I insisted that one night a week we needed to spend time with our friends, and I explained how important it is for me to spend time alone. I needed time to write in my diary, light a candle and some incense and read a book by myself. I needed that quiet time to reflect on my life.

The only problem for us was that in Australia Marc didn't really have his own friends, only those I'd introduced him to. Too much time together eventually resulted in niggling, bickering, and eventually fights. Other challenges arose. Marc walked out of the car yard after falling out with his boss. Money became tighter for us but fortunately I liked my job working a couple of nights a week in a Hare Krishna restaurant, so I picked up a couple more shifts. But Marc found it hard to get other work as every possible employer wanted experience, down to cleaners and nut-shellers at the nearby macadamia farms. Tommy invited Marc to go back up to the Gold Coast to work. He'd sold his house on the mountain and came to stay with us for a few days before he moved down to the coast. Times were a-changing again. After dinner one night, Tommy and Marc took a break from playing guitar so we could watch the evening news. We saw the warplanes flying over Afghanistan, and Tommy startled us by slamming his fist down on the table.

'Now we've stuck our neck out,' said Tommy suddenly. 'Now Australia's involved in this whole bloody thing. It'll come back at us, you can bet.'

With the loss of his miserable job at the car yard, Marc had also lost his car. When I needed to use the van for work or uni, Marc was stuck a good ten minute drive from anywhere with nothing but a little pink shopping bike for transport. A man needs to work, and when he cannot find any, he will become bored and frustrated. It was horrid coming home after another stimulating day at uni to find Marc slumped on the couch in front of the Playstation. I was now working at the restaurant for four or five nights a week and attending uni four days a week. I didn't mind, but Marc found himself disempowered, dependent and stranded. 'I miss Dave the Rave,' he said, holding up a picture of Dave standing in his kitchen dressed up as Batman for a party he'd decided not to go to. Dave was also missing his bestest dancing buddy.

I was so tired from working late that getting up early for a surf became difficult, and so our one escape together waned. I was on overdrive, Marc was on slow-mo and we were both gradually going mad.

To make things worse, we were having major issues with my parents and this was putting a lot of strain on our relationship. Dad was being very stubborn, refusing to get a job, which was winding up Mum. To protect my relationship with Marc I tried to create more space between her and us, which only caused further problems. We refused to spend Christmas with my parents, choosing to eat our roast dinner under the fig tree in 40° heat, which wasn't much fun either. Just before New Years Mum burst into our house uninvited and hysterical, demanding why we were being so cruel, and Marc had to ask her to leave.

I cannot remember exactly when my interest for our garden waned, or when the Nutshed became gradually messier and messier as we both cared a little less for our future in that place. It was little more than a season before the garden became neglected, and the weeds began to flourish. The parrots picked at our fallen tomatoes and we let them.

We did have one respite, and that was my uni friend Andy who lived just up the lane. Andy had a tall and wiry frame, with dark Nepalese skin and a floppy mop of thick black hair. He'd recently split up with his long term girlfriend and right afterwards had his heart stomped on by a young German bombshell. Andy was now in recovery and needing shelter and friendship, and we were in need of a friend too. He became rather a fixture over those last few months in the Nutshed, surfing with us as much as possible. I often went out and left them to their boys' nights in, relieved that Marc had a companion other than me.

Marc suggested going back to Cornwall where he had his friends, and I had mine; where we both had separate identities but could still be together. It made sense. I read our tarot cards, asking 'shall we stay or shall we go?' This was the big question, because something had to give. They showed our emotional stagnation, and Marc's disappointment in how things were going for us, with all the hopes he'd held for Australia. They also showed our determination to take on obstacles together, yet there was some uncertainly for our future. The cards had said some strange things, but we took them to mean what we already knew: It was time to give our little home away.

Andy's ex-girlfriend moved in to the Nutshed and we moved all our stuff to my parent's attic. We had a massive garage sale, sold our orange lava-lamp, our fluffy TV and Mousy the Lite-Ace, gathering enough money for one-way tickets back to England. Ironically, things seemed to finally get better where we were after we had bought the tickets, but it was too late. We were going 'home'.

Chapter 5

A Pack of Cards

IT WASN'T *ALL* bad, and it started off just fine. Marc stayed at Carole and Ray's house in Carnon Downs so he could catch up with his family and sort out getting his rusty Corolla back on the road. I wanted to see Gran as soon as possible, so Ray drove me back through the lanes to the village in his red BMW. I asked to go straight down to Chapel Porth, my most special place.

At high tide the wild and rugged beach appears to be a tiny, rocky cove with high waves rebounding off black cliffs. As they crash on the shore, stones are dragged noisily seawards with each retreating wave. The only vegetation on the cliffs is hardy low heather and gorse bushes, which make the valley glow with purple and gold. A few blue-grey mining slag piles stick out of the valley sides like big pimples upon which the arsenic forbids any plant growth. On the valley floor a small stream cuts a narrow course through the heather, winding down from greener wooded banks farther up. As you look out to sea, a rugged granite outcrop perches on the top of the northern head-land, and to the left a large hill rises from the top of the grey-black cliff like a giant cup-cake (as a child I named it cup-cake hill). Large seagulls fly high above, swooping into the cold water with the hope of bringing up a meal of tasty mackerel.

I love Chapel Porth on high tide, but the true magic comes when the tide draws out six hundred metres to reveal the wide stretch of sand and the rocks, wave-worn into all sorts of fascinating shapes. On low tide you can walk along the sand to Porthtowan. As a child this place was a haven for the imagination. To me, each cave was either a palace or a deep, dark witches' den. A pointy rock that rises out of the sand in the middle of the beach has two thrones cut out for a princess and her prince. A natural Jacuzzi is scoured into the rock like a monster shark-bite where you can sit as the waves of the incoming tide wash around you. When the tide draws out farther, there are countless deep and winding caves and I know them all intimately, some as big as cathedrals. Some have big rocks stuck in the entrance that you have to wriggle under to get through, avoiding the barnacles. Others are joined by secret passageways hidden in the black dripping walls. I always loved to show visitors the labyrinth of caves, running off into one, disappearing into the darkness and reappearing somewhere down the beach with a cheeky cackle. As a teenager I gave a tour of the caves to a cute boy that I liked, and it was only in the darkness at the back of the cool damp cave that I could finally pluck up the courage for my first kiss.

My excitement ran high as we turned the bend into Chapel Porth. I smiled at Ray in anticipation. As a ruined engine house disappeared behind the hill we descended the narrow road that ran along the valley side towards the beach. Finally, as we turned into the car park I could read the Chapel Porth sign, made out of a formation of painted white rocks that sat upon the gorse across the valley (I took my turn to paint those once). I'd known the lifeguards at Chapel Porth all my life, and wondered how long it would take for the word to get out that I was back. As we drove past the lifeguard hut I could see Turnip's head follow us as Ray turned the car around. It was about mid-tide with the waves lapping up between the headlands. I saw Turnip smile and turn to his mate. That was all it took and I knew. His mate Tony was on the phone to his girlfriend Nic, who was lifeguarding at Aggie beach. The village already knew I was back and it took about a minute.

I turned up at Gran's little bungalow and I can't describe the joy at seeing her tiny frail frame again. As she stared up at me she looked shocked, despite all the phone calls I'd made to make sure she knew I was coming (she was becoming a little forgetful). She was neatly dressed in a red skirt and a white knitted cardigan over a pale yellow top, wearing her dark blue slippers. Her hair was freshly permed into perfect waves. She hugged me tightly, crying, before disappearing into the kitchen. She brought out her steaming shiny red teapot and some biscuits before Ray made his way home, leaving us to it. As we sat by the crackling fire, Gran asked me a thousand questions.

'How long are you back for?'

'Just summer, I think.'

'What about University, are you going to finish your education?'

'Yes, of course. I'm just taking a year out.'

'Hmmm,' she replied, her eyes sparkling knowingly.

It was decided that I would sleep in the fold-out armchair in her tiny living room until I found a room of my own. Once she was satisfied that I knew what I was doing and had a plan, I pulled on a pair of shorts, a blue top and some rainbow socks. I dusted off my old skate deck to whizz down through the one-way system. It was so good to feel the cool air in my hair as I flew down Town Hill into Peterville. Before I turned to go down to Aggie Beach, I popped into the surf shop to say hello to Mary, an Aussie who'd moved to the village years ago.

'Hanabeth! I heard you got back. How are ya?' she asked. I sighed – *of course* she already knew I was back. I skated down through the lushness of Quay Valley to Aggie Beach. At the top I waved to an old man who had been a friend of my Grandfather. Fifty metres further down I waved to the midwife who had been at my birth (and also happened to own the beach); another fifty metres along I waved to a friend who worked in the newsagents. I stopped for a quick chat with a cousin of Lian's, before committing to the final winding stretch to the beach, past yet another friend and Nic's dad Bunty as he drove up the hill, returning their waves as I weaved my way down the gentle slope. A bloke with a handle bar moustache and long white hair stood with his mates outside the Driftwood, holding up his pint as he smiled and waved.

'All right, Hanabeth?' he called out in a gentle Cornish accent. I flew past giving him the thumbs up, returning the smile and chuckling at their slightly startled expressions. I carved a couple more turns before I crouched and turned up onto the road that veers left towards Trevaunance Point. Finally losing my speed a couple of speed-bumps up the hill, I stepped off to walk back down a steep path to the ocean's edge.

After popping by to see Nic and the other lifeguards, I walked up a steep and narrow road called Rocky Lane and skated over to The Croft, Lian's family home. Everybody was there except Lian. Hugh, her youngest brother had just finished school and now towered above me. We fondly nicknamed Hugh the BFG. He is the tallest member of the Doble family, yet has the kindest, softest heart, and I always felt protective of Huey. He greeted me first, giving me a big bear hug. I saw Mawgan next, the middle sibling who was now back from uni 'upcountry' where he was studying Philosophy (and girls). Where he had once been a grumpy teenager, he was now mellowing into a friendly and interesting adult. He too greeted me with a warm smile and a hug. Unfortunately, Lian was working upcountry. I would have to wait to catch up with her.

I walked around the beautiful Doble house, enjoying the overwhelming sense of safety and warmth. I stood in the high-roofed hallway as sunlight streamed in through the plentiful windows and skylights. The house is always clean, but in summer the constant trail of family, cousins and friends leaves a homely trail of coats piled up in the cloakroom, with shoes, boots, riding hats and beanies spread on the floor.

Jenny and Ian came in from the garden to greet me. Jenny was looking healthy and slim with her curly brown hair cut short. Ian's disappearing-reappearing beard had reappeared. His red-brown bristles were starting to go grey.

I received a kiss from Jenny and a bear-hug from Ian. 'So, how was Australia?' Jenny asked.

'Good, I'm enjoying uni ... but I took a year out to come back here.'

'Okay,' said Jenny, her eyes questioning. 'Are you planning on going back?'

'Yes, definitely. I re-start back at uni in July next year.' Her eyes narrowed. Apart from being a psychologist, Jenny knew me only too well.

'And how are things going with Marc?' My gaze flicked out of the window and I took a sudden interest in the hydrangeas.

'Yeah, good, good. We've overdosed on each other a little bit ... but now we're back here he has plenty of friends to catch up with so should be happier.' Jenny nodded but frowned slightly. We stood chatting by the big old Aga stove that ensured that the house was always kept warm – even in the bleakest, coldest winter days.

Gran put me up as best as she could, treating me like a princess, waking me up to bacon and eggs, tea and sugared grapefruit. Each evening I came back to a home cooked meal, whether it be plaice and mashed potato or salad and potatoes, baked in the glowing coals of the hearth. Marc stayed at Carole and Ray's and found himself a job as a waiter and barman at the 'Blue Bar' in Porthtowan. He was much happier dealing with dirty beer glasses than sump oil and, besides, he was making better money. In Marc's absence I set to work getting back into my old Aggie routine. I went out to the Driftwood with Nic to drink far too many pints of cider and blackcurrant, and proceeded to dance around to a local band until the landlady chucked everybody out. When she started to spray us with air freshener we knew it was time to go to a party. We drank more, danced more and smoked a few spliffs before finally wandering back up through the village to crawl into bed in the small hours.

After I'd quietly crept in one morning and turned on the light, I heard a door creak in the corridor. 'Oh no! I've disturbed Gran. She's gonna be cross,' I thought, jumping in under the covers with my clothes on.

The door opened slowly and Gran peered in. She was in her nighty and pink dressing gown, her grey curls slightly flat on one side of her head.

'Oh, hello love, where've you been?'

'Down at the Driftwood.'

She rolled her eyes disapprovingly, but smiled all the same. 'Not drunk I hope. Would you like a cup of cocoa?'

'That would be lovely!' I grinned, a bit surprised at the offer. I struggled to sit up straight and took off my platform trainers. She brought the cocoa out in little china teacups. As I took the cup, she handed me a silver spoon.

'Make sure it's all stirred in,' she said, as we sat together, our spoons clink-clinking against the side of our cups. A 1960s lampshade bathed the little room in a warm amber light.

'This is just like in the war,' Gran said.

'Really?'

'Yes, up in the middle of the night, all cosy and together with a cup of cocoa.' She smiled fondly. I wondered how she could feel nostalgic about such a time.

I slept in until around midday and then hung out down the beach all day, surfing a couple of times. In the Cornish sunshine, it's pretty fine to wear a bikini as long as you keep paddling around. I walked back up the hill to Gran's place and found Marc waiting for me.

'Hey babe.' He kissed me. 'How are you settling in?'

'Good. It's cool to be back. Gran's a legend. I joined the surf club too. I want to get my NARS.'

'Eh? What's a NARS?'

'You know, for lifeguarding, like the old Bronze, like I told you before.'

'Ah yep, yep. Good on you, babe.' He grabbed my hand.

'How's life with the folks?' I asked.

'Lovely as ever. They do spoil me. They're so happy we're back! Wanna go down the Driftwood for dinner?'

'Sure.' I smiled. We walked down to the beach past the Aggie Hotel, following the one-way system past the tall steeple of the Church and down Town Hill, turning off to go past a row of rickety old miner's cottages, so steeply and precariously perched almost upon each other that they featured in many post-cards and were famously known as Stippy Stappy. Our hands swung together as we wove through the network of footpaths down to the beach. We walked into the Driftwood and chose the same table we had sat at on Nic's birthday almost two years before. Marc got up to order some food and then I heard it... Marc had stopped dead in his tracks. He turned back towards me and then we both looked over to the far end of the bar where my Mother was sitting with some friends and laughing. Marc came and sat back down slowly. I spoke first:

'We've been back *four* days, what is *she* doing here?'

Marc shook his head in disbelief. 'Let's get out of here.'

I soon had two jobs. Sadly, my old teapot scrubbing job could be no more, as Trevaunance Point Hotel was no more, transformed from the run down old hotel with its adorable drunken owner, to a million pound private house and holiday flats. One of the managers had started up her own restaurant in the top of the village called Sally's, and my old friend the hotel chef had moved there. We'd always gotten on well, so I was stoked to work with him again and enjoyed his continual friendly piss-taking (mostly out of me). My other job was right on the beach, waitressing in Schooners next to the beach huts. It was now run by a boy I'd gone to school with, whose father once lifeguarded with my dad.

Our next task was to find a room somewhere. We went round to Wiseacres to see the family there, but of course our old room was filled. Another family friend had a room that had just become available in her downstairs granny flat. The room had a bed, a couch, a bench, and looked across a green valley with an old engine house on the top. It was the same engine house that I could see from my bedroom when I was growing up. In the next room lived a lovely bubbly friend who worked down at the Driftwood, called Malarie. We moved our stuff in. Marc and I decided that we would live there together, but Marc stressed that he would need some space too, which was fine by me. Or so I thought.

It didn't take long for things to go downhill, and it started with car insurance. I was so longing for some independence that summer and I'd never had a license in Cornwall before. In England, insurance is a tricky and expensive deal. Marc organised insurance for his old Corolla, but without my name on the policy. It sounds like a small thing but it was so out of character for him not to think of me, and meant I couldn't drive the car we were supposed to be sharing. In fact, it was the first warning sign of trouble ahead.

We could only afford one-way flights to the UK so we wanted to make sure that we had our escape back sorted out before winter overtook us. I booked us flights for the second of October to Bali. We had to pay upfront, so Gran helped us out and we paid her back over the summer. We had our future mapped out, but the seeds of doubt soon took root, and the carefully assembled pack of cards started to shake.

The following Monday was Nicola's birthday, and the second anniversary of our first kiss. We had celebrated every other six-month anniversary, but this time, well, we didn't. Anyone from our part of Cornwall knows that Monday is pound a pint night at The Loft in Truro. I was having a girls' night out, mainly because Marc insisted he didn't like the Loft. It turned into a huge night involving tequila, champagne, much dancing and several spliffs. It was a lot of fun but I was glad to finally get home somewhere around 2:30.

As I walked up the short road to our new place I looked forward to crawling into bed with Marc. Only he wasn't there. Odd… I waited for a bit. Another night owl, Malarie, was up so I went in to have a smoke with her. She said that she'd seen Marc hanging out with a few girls down the Driftwood, including a younger girl called Naomi. They had gone back to her house in Peterville for a smoke, about 200 metres down the road. I pictured Naomi, a beautiful tall girl with long straight dark hair and gorgeous eyes who played guitar, and was an amazing singer. I shrugged it off.

'Hmm, a bit odd,' I said casually.

'I'm sure you've nothing to worry about,' said Malarie, but the sympathy still showed in her eyes. Eventually I went to bed, but as time wore on I grew less sure. I tossed and turned. Sleep became impossible as the worry magnified with every moment that passed. I got up after about half an hour and went back into Malarie's room. She was sat on her bed listening to David Gray, smoking another reefer.

'Sorry to disturb you, but I'm going mad! It's four am and he's still not back. What do I do?' My eyebrows lowered, showing a worry I had never experienced before.

'Yeah…it's getting pretty late now. Has he ever done this before?'

'No. Nothing like this. Not ever,' I replied.

'Well, I'll walk down with you if you want to sort this out.' Feeling pathetic, I nodded. I *had* to see, so we walked down to the house. Several lights were on in different rooms.

Who knows what I was planning to do when I got to the house? Knock on the door at four in the morning? I didn't even *know* these people. Maybe I was going to look in through the window to see Marc.

'Which is her bedroom?' I whispered to Malarie.

'Hmm, I'm not sure, maybe that one?' She pointed to a lit-up window out on the top floor. But as she pointed, the light went out and Marc did not emerge. Panic rose in my heart as I turned and ran home. My fears had been confirmed – the lovers had seen me. I lay wide awake, imagining a thousand awful things that Marc could be up to, my mind spinning out of control.

By the time Marc walked in at 6am the sun was already illuminating the grey sky. From the doorway I watched the trees on the hill blowing wildly. My surfboard was under my arm. I couldn't bear to wait any longer and I had to do *anything* to get away from there, and surfing was all I had. I stood with damp eyes as I watched him walk sheepishly up the concrete steps into the garden. He stopped in front of me, looking guilty.

'I'm walking to Chapel Porth.' I barely recognised my own stony voice. I could not look him in the eye.

'What's wrong?' he asked, appearing confused.

'What's wromg?! It's 6 in the morning! What do you expect me to think?!' I cried angrily. I stormed through the garden, down the steps and started walking down the street. Marc followed me, running backwards.

'Come on. Let's talk about this. Let me give you a lift,' Marc pleaded.

'I'm fine. Piss off,' I replied through my tears.

'Oh, come on. Let me at least give you a lift and explain.'

It was a long way, and would take me an hour to walk. I was furious but also curious to hear what he had to say, so I pushed my board into the back of his car and jumped in.

It was a silent ten-minute drive. As we pulled up in the empty car park overlooking the sea, I jumped out and carried my board onto the beach. The surf was about two foot and wildly choppy, breaking on the rocks at high tide. There was nothing to surf, and not even the lifeguards would be down there for another four hours. I had nowhere else to go, and the tears were streaming down my face. I sat on a broad rock facing the ocean. Marc sat down next to me as we both stared at the waves rushing over the rocks and sucking back only metres from us.

'Nothing happened! *Honestly!*' he pleaded.

'I don't believe you.' I glanced at Marc, alarmed to see that blood was gushing out of his nose (I'd never known him to have a nosebleed before).

'What happened?' I asked, suddenly concerned.

'I don't know, it just started a second ago.' He was obviously very upset too. 'I haven't had this since school. Look, Hanabeth, honestly, it sounds weird I know, but there were four of us there smoking and we just kept talking, drifting in and out of sleep and rolling another smoke. A mess I know, but nothing like *that*. I promise!' Marc attempted a smile as he tried hopelessly to stop the flow of blood with his fingers. The scene was almost comical, and I fought back the urge to laugh blackly. I looked into his eyes, which seemed sincere, and as he talked I found myself starting to believe him. Eventually, I started to feel sorry for *him* as he was clearly upset from seeing me so hurt and angry. He had never seen me that way before, probably because I'd never *been* that way before. I picked up a rock and threw it as far as I could, aiming for a rock pool Marc had been throwing stones into, each one hitting his target. I missed, my rock bouncing down onto the caramel coloured sand.

'Okay,' I said finally. 'I believe you, let's go home.'

'I do need my space, Hanabeth,' Marc said. I looked across at him, exasperated. He was sitting on the bed as I poured milk on my Weetabix, standing in the kitchen outside the bedroom door. It was about a week later, and I had noticed Marc spending a bit more time with Naomi. She was a good guitarist and they liked to jam together. It made me a little uneasy in my stomach but I couldn't see anything actually wrong with it, except that I could feel Marc distancing himself from me. She was a very pretty girl, after all, and I knew just how persuasive young girls could be.

'Well, *you* have somewhere to go!' I responded. 'Just go and have your space. This is my *home!* You can stay at your parents and have your space from me,' I replied, carrying the bowl into the bedroom. Something in Marc's eyes made me realise I was not understanding him somehow. He looked frustrated. That night was the first night we had both had off work for a while. I was trying to synchronise a night or two off at the same time as Marc each week, he didn't seem to have bothered sorting it out with his work. Should I have read the signs? We decided that we would watch a video with Malarie, and I sat down next to him on the couch.

Before the opening credits were through Naomi burst into the room in tears. She had broken up with her boyfriend. Marc got straight up to give her a big hug and I could instantly see they'd become close. Why had she come here and not her best mate's place, which was *two minutes* away? I stood up to comfort her as I thought I should, but felt cool towards her, confused at the apparent level of intimacy between them. Marc sat back down and, to my horror, patted the couch next to him while smiling at Naomi. I sat alone in the armchair, feeling confused. Okay, so she needs some attention, but this is *weird,* I thought. I could see her admiration for Marc with her beautiful big brown puppy dog eyes.

'No big deal,' I said firmly to myself, so I sat on the floor in front of Marc as I had done hundreds of times, and put my head on his lap. It would usually have been the most natural thing, but this felt strange. No hands came to caress my head or run through my hair. He made no attempt to touch me, so eventually I sat back in the chair and watched the film to the end with a chilly feeling inside.

Was I being silly? I asked Malarie the next morning.

'Yeah, it does seem a bit odd,' she replied. I spoke to Marc, trying to carefully explain that I was feeling a bit jealous, and I had never felt that before. I said I knew it was silly, but asked him to maybe be a bit more thoughtful. I was surprised at his response:

'Look, I just need my space at the moment,' he said bluntly. He was preparing to drive to the nearby city of Truro, and I had stuff to do in there.

'Can I come with you?' I asked. It *was* an hour-long bus trip. Marc was hesitant but agreed. I instantly wished I hadn't asked as I felt as if I was tagging along and intruding on his space. I sat down in the passenger seat. Before he started the car I was surprised to see him dial a number on his phone.

'Good morning Naomi, do you fancy coming into Truro?' At this point I was making wild hand signals and mouthing: 'NO!' I was horrified. Had he not heard a word I'd said? As he hung up, I looked at him in bewilderment.

'What the hell!' I raised my voice to a shrill pitch. 'One minute ago I was asking you to be more careful with my heart, and now you are asking her along with us??' Marc's reaction surprised me: he was angry.

'Just fuck off and leave me alone!' he shouted.

I felt like a stalker. 'Fine! It's over. Forget it,' I shouted back, slamming the car door.

'Fine by me,' he replied, and drove away.

Chapter 6

Snakes and Ladders

FROM THEN ON, the events of that summer all just sort of jumble together. I stopped eating properly, which had never happened to me before. Each day I ate two Weetabix with milk at around lunchtime and then forced down a couple of mouthfuls of dinner after work at Sally's. Marc and I spoke a day or so after the breakup. I think Marc may even have stayed in Naomi's sister's room while she was away (how convenient). Had *I* driven them together with my jealousy? I'd lost all comprehension of what was going on in Marc's head or heart. A few days later we agreed to try and stagger our nights at our rented room. I would stay at my mates' places for a few days, while Marc had the room, and then Marc could stay at his folks for a few days when I had the room, so we gave each other the space he kept talking about.

I stayed at the Dobles for a few nights, and on Friday it was my turn to try to sleep in our room. I walked up the hill towards the house and I was already in a state, crying because of something silly, panicking really. I had my life-guard exam the next day but could not get the night off work and I had done no study at all so far. When I noticed Marc's car was parked on the road outside, there was a minor improvement in my mood. Still, I was a pathetic sight as I entered the room crying. I stopped in my tracks, staring in disbelief. Who should be there with Marc, but Naomi? They were just sitting there, but in my state I couldn't handle it. I turned on my heels and walked straight upstairs without a word, coming back down one minute later to find them gone. My heart sank as angry tears flowed down my cheeks. I picked up a beautiful picture of Marc and I that Ray had taken at Broken Head one glorious morning. I held it in my hands, thinking how far we were from that beauty now. In my rage, I tore it right down the middle before throwing it on the floor. I washed my face and went to work in tears. Seeing the state I was in, Chef was nice to me, leaving me alone to wash dishes in the corner. Afterwards, I pulled a scarf around my head and left, still crying hopelessly.

Pushing my emotions out of my head, I stayed up late cramming for the NARS exam, hastily filling out the file full of whatever knowledge I had to know, memorising the blood system, bandaging techniques and the different varieties of shock. My exam started at eight so I woke up early and skated down to the beach faster than I ever had before, my big backpack on my back.

'Fuck it,' I muttered as I pushed off from the top of the big hill, bracing myself for some speed, crouching slightly. I figured that as it was early there'd be no cars. By the time I passed the Driftwood, I was usually going slow enough to jump off, but there was no jumping this time – I was going far too fast for that. To my horror, down the road I saw a red car reversing out of the side road up to Trevaunance Point, which was my slow down ramp. The only other option was an extremely abrupt slope down to the beach, with high stony walls on either side. I yelled out to the driver of the red hatchback, but they didn't hear or see me approaching fast. They were reversed almost right up to the pavement as I sped closer, leaving only the tiniest gap. The pavement was high and I had only a mini-skirt and jumper on. My options were either to jump, hit the car anyway and get mashed on the gravel, or hope. I hoped, and made myself as skinny as I could as I approached the gap that was now barely a foot wide. I focused on a point up the hill, and as if by magic I found myself zooming up the road towards the Point, blinking. I was nearly at the hotel at the top of the hill when the wheels finally ran out of momentum. With my knees wobbling, I kicked a 180 turn and glided slowly back down the gradual slope. The car drove off, oblivious to the whole event. There was an old man in his garden at the house opposite the turning. Holding his spade, he had frozen still, but his eyes were following me. I stepped off to talk to him.

'I have no idea how you fit through that gap,' he said, shaking his head in amazement. All I could do was shake my head in reply, with my eyebrows raised, pulling a strange face.

Feeling pretty shaky, I wobbled the last twenty metres to my exam. As I arrived at one minute past eight, about twelve people stood waiting at the Surf Club. I was on automatic pilot as I swam out in the waves and carried out my rescues, my lifts, CPR and first aid tests. Only half the group passed, and somehow I was the only girl who did. Feeling somewhat proud of my achievement, I walked back up the hill to the flat, having almost forgotten about the night before.

When I got home the biggest shock yet was in store for me. Marc's stuff was gone – all of it. His skateboard was gone from where it had rested by the front door; his sunnies were gone from the bench; the drawers were empty of his clothes; his toothbrush was missing from the glass next to the sink. He'd been through our CD case and removed every single one of his CDs. All he left was a photograph and a note that simply said, 'Fuck you'. The photograph was a passport photo of me he'd carried around in his wallet for two years, ripped into shreds. I lay down on the bed in desolation, a sickness rising in my stomach and a cold, cold feeling embedding itself in my whole body.

At Schooners, I interacted with people as little as possible while staring out at the wind-whipped grey waves of the cove. I watched the tide rise and fall, rise and fall, then rise and fall again as time became meaningless. I served coffee, took money, dropped dishes off in the kitchen and brought out plates of food, yet I had never felt less like eating. In my break I scribbled a poem on the back of an old menu. All I felt was desolation, and only the written word seemed to relieve some of my pain. Even my diet of Weetabix was a struggle to place in my mouth. Laurs and I worked together, and we sat down together for a cup of tea after the restaurant closed.

'Hb, I'm really worried about you,' she said as she pulled her blonde hair free from her ponytail. 'You're just not yourself at the moment. Are you eating?'

'Yes...well I'm trying to. Everything tastes like cardboard. I can barely eat Weetabix any more. That's all I've been able to eat. I'm trying to have dinner each day, but I've lost my appetite.'

'Weetabix? U-huh. Wait a sec...' She got up and went into the kitchen for a couple of minutes, and returned with a small bowl of steaming broth. 'Do you like seafood chowder?' she asked kindly.

'Normally, yes,' I responded. 'I can certainly try...I know I *should* be hungry.' I sipped at a few spoonfuls, feeling the thick, warm liquid sinking into my abandoned tummy. It tasted pretty good. 'Thanks Laurs, this is good stuff.' She looked back at me and nodded, smiling sympathetically.

'Are you sleeping?' she asked next.

'Barely...' I looked at the floor. 'Its funny, I've now gotten the figure I've always wanted, yet *all I want to be is happy and fat!*' I was deadly serious, but we both broke into laughter all the same, as tears ran down my face.

I walked up past the old hotel to Trevaunance Point. On the edge of the rocky cliff I took some deep breaths, watching the waves crash on the rocks far below as the sea spray swept around me. Seagulls squawked as they spun in winding circles above and below. It started to rain, so I pulled my black coat tightly around me and sat on a ledge, tears falling from my eyes directly into the seething ocean far below.

Eventually Marc came around to see me. I looked down from the window to see his car pull in to my old driveway in the pouring rain. He looked up at me through the window, and indicated he wanted to take me for a drive. We watched the rain pour down the windscreen, distorting the world into a blurred, dancing water colour painting as we drove through the lanes.

'What's happening to you, babe?' I asked finally.

'I don't know. I just need this time,' he replied, shrugging his shoulders and staring ahead, his eyes on the road, both hands firmly on the wheel. I watched his profile and wondered how things could get better, and whether they would.

'How much time do you *need*?'

'I don't know. Just give me a few weeks. I can come and see you once or twice a week.' I considered his offer, and decided to support him.

'Well, if that's what you need... I guess.' I sighed a deep sigh. This wasn't going to be over for a while. 'What *is* going on with Naomi?'

'Nothing. We're friends, we play music together.'

'I saw you together at the Driftwood yesterday.' Marc stopped the car on the cliff top, breaking a bit too abruptly. He turned to look at me.

'Look. You've got nothing to worry about. She's too young anyway! If you want something to worry about look at this!' He handed me a card and a copy of the 'Blue Day Book,' a little book full of cute photos of animals and cheesy life affirmations. I opened the card and read the neat hand-writing. It was signed 'Your Hot Chicky,' and had a suggestive note written on the inside cover. Too confused to be hurt, I looked up at Marc.

'What the hell is this, and why are you showing it to me? How long has this been going on?' I spoke pretty calmly, considering.

'It's not going on! She just has a crush on me. She won't leave me alone. She stalks me at the Blue Bar. Her nickname's 'Nutty Nicky'. She's crazy.' Marc shrugged his shoulders and I drew a breath, wondering how on earth to take this.

I sighed wearily. '*Your Hot Chicky*? I don't know if I know you at all anymore.'

The following months were like a game of snakes and ladders. We would take one step forwards and then two steps back. We saw each other once or twice a week, but mainly Marc stayed between Porthtowan and Carnon Downs, avoiding the village, avoiding me too I guess. Our arguments were heated and frequent. Often they would involve my mother as I realised that some sort of peace would have to be found with her, but Marc had run out of patience. I'd seen her around, but still hadn't felt like talking to her. I don't think she had any idea of the role she had played in our leaving Australia, and I knew she wasn't likely to acknowledge that perhaps it had not been so great to turn up at our house screaming and uninvited. Those scars were still fresh for Marc and I. There had been lots of reasons we left, but I couldn't help but feel that if family life had been more supportive than destructive, we may not have felt such a strong need to run away. Still, although she wasn't perfect, she *was* my mother after all, and had a lot of good points (setting the drama aside). On a beautiful warm summer's eve Mum had given me two tickets to see St. Agnes Players perform *A Midsummer Night's Dream* beside the ruins of an ivy-covered old engine house on the hillside. Marc didn't want to come so I brought Nic along. Both our mums were sat opposite us, and I gave Mother a nod of recognition. I thought that was generous.

Somehow, between the arguments, Marc and I shared some idyllic days. We surfed up the coast and visited Timbo and Polly, only to find that they'd split up, and Timbo was on the move again. In fact, by pure chance he was booked to go to Bali on the same flight as us.

We had one day of heaven down at Perran Sands, where we'd had our first date. As we stood on the top of the dune, solid lines of green swell moved slowly landwards from the horizon, rising up and peeling across the beach. We picked our spot to paddle out through the wide surf zone to where the green water twinkled in the summer light. Neither Marc nor I wore our wetsuits, warmed by the midday sun and refreshed by the cool waters of the Atlantic.

Marc paddled for a set wave and rode the clear green wall right to the sand, carving turns on his longboard, walking casually up the board with his hands behind his back.

'I almost got to the nose!' he cried with a flash of a smile as he sat back up on his board next to us. 'Soon!' he said, 'I'll get there.'

'I know you will, babe!' I encouraged.

It was a rare, warm, sunny day and after our surf we sat at the base of the dunes with our skin touching. I can still smell the surf wax and the saltiness of our sun-kissed skin, the softness of my cheek on his chest, his wet hair on my fingertips. I remember the shape of our surfboards leaning on the dune, his long, green board with its red fin next to my small rainbow swallow-tail. The tide was coming in, and the summer was racing fast to a close. Days like this are few and far between in Cornwall. In fact, days like this are few and far between in life.

On the way home we brought strawberries, raspberries and clotted cream, taking a scenic route that cut through the deep valley in tunnels of green trees. Spotting a half-hidden gateway, we pulled up and climbed over the wooden gate and sat in the long green grass looking down the valley. Marc spoke first:

'I love that you can roll about in the grass with no worry of spiders, ants, snakes and ticks.'

'Hmmm,' I responded dreamily, opening the raspberries. Marc popped a strawberry loaded with cold, thick cream in to my mouth.

'Why can't it always be this easy?' Marc asked.

'It should be,' I answered. For half a second Marc frowned, but it was soon replaced by his wide smile as I popped a strawberry into his mouth. We moved closer together in the light of the afternoon sun. I touched his soft skin, almost crying with how much I had missed this intimacy. We knew each other's bodies so well, and the electric kiss was still there. We watched the evening bend the sunlight into a hazy orange over the hills. Too soon, we had to get back in the car to go to our evening shifts.

Within days, the magic was broken again, and I struggle to remember exactly why. Maybe I asked to see him the next day and he changed once more, brushed me off with an excuse. Maybe I pushed too much. Maybe we were both working too much with shifts that clashed, or maybe he was with another girl? I'll never know.

The final straw was on the evening of the SAS Ball.

'Will you come and get ready with me?' I asked, smiling.

'Ah, well the guys from the Blue Bar are having a kinda pre-party.'

'Okay, it would be nice to hang out together,' I pushed, almost pleading. 'It is *The Ball*,'

'Look, I want to spend some time with them, then I will come and pick you up and we can go together!'

'Okay then, I'll get ready at the Doble's and see you then … No worries.'

I stood with Lian at Jenny's bathroom mirror, sprinkling 'fairy dust' across our cheek-bones and fixing my pixie ears in place, getting ready for the 'Creatures of the Enchanted Forest' SAS Ball. I fixed in place a pale blue wig, wearing a gown woven with silver and rainbow thread.

'What do you think?' Lian asked excitedly. I took a step back and giggled. She was green from head to toe.

'Ha ha! You look great. What exactly *are* you again?'

'We are Sprites Against Sewage, *Hanabeth!* I told you before,' she scolded in mock anger.

'Of course you are. Sorry!' I smiled. The Doble ritual for the SAS Ball was that each year the whole family would wear a different coloured body paint for the cause. At the Fire Ball they were Satans Against Sewage; at the Glow Ball they'd been Statues Against Sewage and the year before that they had been Smurfs Against Sewage. Whatever the theme, I knew there would always be a large group of cousins dressed in the matching outfits they created together with painstaking attention to detail.

Brushing some mascara across my eyelashes, I was ready to go.

'Do I look alright?' I asked Lian.

'You look fab!' she replied, gently brushing a speck of glitter from my left eyelash. We went downstairs to have a drink with the family and their extensive entourage. After a while, everybody was piling into cars to take the short drive round the Beacon to the Ball. I was offered a lift each time a car drove away. As the last few walked out, Lian paused by the door and looked back at me:

'Are you *sure* you don't want to come with us?'

'Oh, no, I'll wait for Marc. He won't be long.' I smiled. Lian looked back not entirely satisfied.

'Well, okay, I'll see you there then. Are you *sure* he's coming?' I looked at her, surprised at her lack of faith in Marc.

'Of course he is!' I said indignantly. Hugging her goodbye, I realised her doubt was not so surprising. I'd been crying on her shoulder the whole time she'd been home.

Suddenly the house was very quiet, so I waited in the kitchen with the dogs. And I waited, and I waited some more. I tried to call Marc but his phone kept going straight to voicemail. Feeling frustrated and abandoned, I started to cry, smudging my carefully applied makeup.

Finally, a light flickered in the window as some headlights lit the driveway. I walked outside. Whatever excuse he had was simply not going to measure up. I glared at him as I got in the car. I didn't even give him a chance to speak.

'This is crazy! Where have you *been*?' I asked angrily, all my frustration, jealousy and rage ready to burst.

'Just down at the Blue Bar having some drinks with my mates…'

'Yeah, and Nutty Nicky too I bet. Well, it's just *not* good enough any more. I thought that we would go to the ball together with the Dobles… They left at eight-thirty and like an *idiot* I've been waiting for you!'

'Well, that's pretty early…' Marc replied. Losing all control I started to scream at him. An unfamiliar beast was unleashed.

'Yes, but now it's *ten-thirty*! This is nuts. I've been wait-ing here by myself as you *please* yourself once again! I'm sick of this, you selfish asshole! You just don't care about me *at all* anymore do you? This relationship is shit, and I'm over it.'

'You're just so clingy!' he responded angrily. 'You just never let me be! You have to have *control all* of the time!'

As we turned into the ball, thousands of people were swarming down towards the big white marquees on the hillside. Coloured lights hit the clouds. Who should be walking down the road but Naomi, looking very beautiful (*perfect* timing).

'We are *not* giving her a lift,' I said to Marc as he slowed down to wave. She smiled and waved back as we drove past. I did not wave. We sat in the car, arguing some more. Eventually we managed to calm down enough to go in, but no sooner had we walked in than we 'lost' each other amongst the crowd of fairies, pixies, wildebeests, dryads and walking magic mushrooms. Every now and then a green Doble sprite tackled me with the aim of making me as green as possible. I laughed and danced, but inside I was wooden, just going through the motions.

The next morning I went for the traditional post-ball sunrise surf. No longer did I want Marc to accompany me, so I paddled out alone in the choppy ocean, allowing myself to get sucked out in the rip past the old ruined harbour. There was some good-sized swell coming through but a decent onshore wind was already blowing the waves into a mess. Turnip and Bunty soon paddled out to catch a few. I nodded a polite greeting, paddling over to my own left-hand peak to catch a few messy close-outs. I jumped off at the end of a ride, my board flying in the air as the wave exploded into a wall of white foam. Somehow it was good medicine, getting washed around underwater, feeling my limbs pulled this way and that, tossed around like a rag doll. I held my breath and relaxed, knowing that the wave would recede and that soon I would be reaching the surface for a fresh breath.

The next afternoon I invited Marc around to the flat. He turned up, silent and solemn. I gestured for him to sit on the couch and sat opposite him on the edge of the bed. My legs were crossed and my arms were folded firmly across my chest.

'What did you want to talk about?' Marc said finally, shuffling uneasily as he tried to read the wooden expression on my face.

'Us,' I replied, blinking.

'What is it?' He looked directly at me.

'I just can't take it anymore, Marc. All of *this*. I can't do this anymore.'

'What do you mean?' he asked in a concerned tone.

'I love you, more than you know, more than anyone I have ever loved.' I glanced at his face, surprised at the cold tone in my voice. 'I want to be with you, but I *can't* take this rubbish anymore. I don't think I even really know who you are any more. The wedge has just grown too big between us. If you don't want to be with me, or if you're still not sure, then I'd rather be on my own. It will hurt like hell, I know, but one day I *will* get over it and I'll find someone who wants to be with me. I deserve that. I'll start again. Don't worry, I'll still be your friend, and I'll support you through the rest of your visa if you want to come back to Australia. That's not long anyway. If you don't want to come, then that's fine too. It's your choice, but we can't be together anymore. It's over now. It's over, Marc.'

He rested his head in his hands and leaned forwards, silent for a long time. When he finally looked up I was surprised to see large tears rolling down his face.

'Hanabeth, you are the *best* girl I have ever met. There is no better girl out there for me. *You* are the best girl for me. I don't want to break up! I love you so, *so* much,'

'Well, why have you treated me this way then!' I cried, with tears now streaming down my own cheeks. I tried hopelessly to stem the flow with my hands.

'I'm so sorry, babe. I didn't realise I'd hurt you so much.' Our eyes were locked again. Marc stood up and reached out his arms from across the room towards me.

'*How could you not see?*' I said quietly.

'I want to get through this *with you,* babe! I want to come with you back to Australia. Let's go to Bali together and we can work through this *together.* Let's make a fresh start. We can make it work. We have to!' We stared at each other for a few moments before he spoke again. 'Will you forgive me? Will you take me back, babe? I don't want this to end.'

I took a huge breath. It was difficult to know what to say. I hadn't expected this. 'Well, if that's how you feel, I would love you to come with me, but I've got to be honest. I've lost my trust in you. It was such a beautiful trust, and I can't get that back over night. It's not going to be easy... but I can try.'

Marc stood and stepped over to me, lifting my chin and kissing me on my forehead, then on my lips, folding his arms around me. Feeling the warmth of his loving arms, some of the cold inside me started to melt, but did not go away.

'Okay,' I whispered, looking up to meet his gaze: 'Let's try again.'

Chapter 7

Ten Days and Twenty-Four Hours

MY HOLIDAY DIARY

2/10/02 Flight QF397

As time goes by I'm getting more and more paranoid about flying. Especially I hate flying without Marc. I know it makes no sense but I can't help the irrational fear that the plane could suddenly explode and leave Marc alone on the ground as I plummet at high speed into the icy ocean.

Well, not so icy actually. I think we are flying over the equator … and right now there's nothing to worry about as Marc is sitting in the seat next to me looking out the window. It's still only his third flight ever and he's pretty excited. Even the silly little plane meals we get with all the little trays and bits of plastic packaging are a novelty to him. He's like a little kid. It's cool to watch him as I've become pretty casual about these things, with this being something like my 50th flight. In fact, when I think about it, my fear of flying only began since I met Marc.

It was so sad to leave Carole, Ray and Steve behind at Gatwick Airport today, but I know that my parents and Tom will be eagerly awaiting our arrival in Australia in just seventeen days time. Mum and Dad's house will be nearly finished when we get back to Byron.

I still remember so clearly the first time I met Carole and Ray. They are everything that I always wanted my parents to be when I was a kid: caring, peaceful and productive, reliable and steadfast. Of course, I love my parents for all that they are, but every kid wants to be 'normal'. It turns out that the very normality of the Gajardos really is what makes them so special. I have come to realise that turmoil and challenge are far more common characteristics of a typical family than normality and stability.

We'll have been together two and a half years before we know it. It's such a shame this Cornish summer has been so testing, but the past is the past, even if it was only a few weeks ago. Now is the time to forget about the past and future. It's time to get back to where and why we started ... right now it's time to play; we're going to Bali. Whoop whoop!

3/10/03 (something hideous am)

The stewardess is taking forever to get to our seat. I'm so hungry. Of course neither of us has caught any sleep on this bloody long flight. The smell of plane food still disgusts me though, wafting about through the stale recycled air. Marc is being silly, acting like he's dying of hunger, or thirst, or lack of alcohol, or all three. I think he's silly sometimes just to avoid thinking about his problems. I mean I do it too, but it's annoying me right now.

I have to admit it is still hard to cast the events of the past few months from my mind. I still need to talk about it. In fact I just tried and it went like this:

'Marc…'

'What?' he replied absent-mindedly.

'Can you promise me…?'

'Hanabeth!' he warned.

'Please… just promise me that you are sure nothing happened with those girls?' I pleaded. Marc flashed an angry look at me:

'Look! I don't want to talk about it! Why can't you just leave it alone! Stop pestering me. It's like two in the morning, let me listen to the CD. I Just want to relax.'

'Marc!' I didn't expect such bad temper, but he went on:

'Leave me alone or I'll catch the first plane back to England when we get there.' He turned his back to me as much as he could in the narrow seat and stared hard out the window, before getting up and muttering that he was going up the aisle to see Timbo.

My heart is thumping inside my chest, our relationship flashing before my eyes. I look up the aisle. I want to knock on the pilot's door and ask him to turn the plane around. The unhealed pain of the summer is welling up in my chest. How can he be so cruel! I have nowhere to run to, but he just can't see what he put me through.

Where did it go wrong? He had made a quick decision to give up everything to come and live in Australia with me, and now look at us! I think Bali will either make or break us.

5/10/03 Legian Inn

The air is humming with activity. I can hear my Balinese Mama rattling around creating something in the kitchen, and the drone of the TV Oka is watching with his niece on the open platform in the middle of the courtyard (Oka owns Legian Inn with his sister Made, who's daughter I used to play with as a toddler). We've got a clean little room with beautiful, hand-crafted, Balinese furniture. There's no air-con but I like having the windows open so I can hear the distant gamelan music playing, and the swish-swish sound of Made sweeping the courtyard before I hear the clink of her dropping off delicious tea for us in the still early morning.

Marc and I have been getting on so much better. We keep talking through stuff, ironing out the deeper creases each time. He is finally realising that I just need to understand what went on before I can let it slip into the past. And I am starting to understand what was going on in his head this summer. He'd felt out of control in Australia and lost in my world. He'd needed the space to find his own self, without me, before he could commit to coming back to meet the inevitable challenges back in Byron, with me.

The sun has shone every day so far. Marc fell in love with Bali the moment he arrived. We left him with the pile of boards and bags as Timbo and I tried to organise a taxi. We returned to find Marc amongst the chaos of the airport front steps, standing out in his orange pants and yellow t-shirt, with his head thrown back in laughter and his arms above his head.

'I love this place!' he repeated a couple of times as he looked around in wonder. The first thing I did was take Marc for a walk around Kuta. He wants to buy a million things but I told him the first day is the best for getting ripped off.

The first night we went out to dinner with Timbo, Bobby and these other American guys from the San Clemente who all seem pretty cool. It's so good to have food back at Warung Linggar! We ended up at the Sari Club (gggaah!!) as the boys love the place, and what better club to open Marc's eyes to the Bali nightlife. The guys sat around for most of the night drinking Bintangs while Marc and I danced like idiots to exactly the same tunes they were playing when I was last in the Sari Club, like *Land Down Under*, *Cher* and lots of hyper techno shit. Towards the end of the night we even got Bobby dancing (who says he never dances but has every time I've been out with him). I can't wait to go surfing with them. They've left to go off on a boat trip and will be back on Saturday. I wish I could go with them but that would definitely be throwing Marc in the deep end; he hasn't even surfed a reef yet.

117

The surf was pretty small for the first couple of days so we stuck to surfing the beach breaks. I introduced Marc to the beach ladies at Legian where we lay under the shade for an hour after a surf, recieving a slightly sandy massage, drifting back to Legian Inn smelling of coconut oil.

6/10/03 (11 am) Lembongan Island

We stayed at Legian Inn for one night before catching a boat over here yesterday. It's so beautiful here. I never tire of the place despite there being virtually nothing to do except surf. The electricity stops for most of the day so the fan above me is still. I am lying on the bed sweating, looking up at the woven bamboo ceiling and walls of our beachside hut. I stayed at this place once with the worst Bali Belly when Nic and I had the room upstairs … sharing with a rat! Let's hope *he* doesn't live here anymore.

Yesterday afternoon it was a really low tide so we walked out to the old shipwreck to take a look at the reef. My idea was to show Marc that there was nothing to worry about, but it didn't work! It was a total mission, walking for 500 meters across the short pegs and string of the seaweed farms. Marc complained the place looked barren and unhealthy, unimpressed by the state of the reef. When we got back I bumped into Nyoman on the beach who showed me a beautiful turtle he'd caught to have for dinner. I felt so sad and tried to dissuade him but it is their tradition. I suppose I have to respect that, but it's still a challenge seeing the beautiful turtle with his fins tied together.

After a tiny surf at Shipwrecks this morning, Marc and I hired a knackered old bike and did one thing I've always wanted to do: drive round the island! There are all these villages that are totally traditional, shaky bamboo huts, with tiny shops selling only peanuts and a few glass bottles of sprite and coke. They say they sent all the crazy people from Bali out to Lembongan, years ago. The villagers smiled bright red smiles from the betel nut they chew, waving as we drove by; they obviously don't see white people much on this side of the island.

I think we are both remembering why we got together in the first place. Marc is just so stoked on life, and we share that. I can't think of many people who giggle as much as we do. Some people might call us childish and maybe we are, but so what?! Here in Bali our problems have dissolved. Now they seem pale and insignificant. What *did* we ever fight about anyway?!

7/10/03 Legian Inn

It's sooooo good to be back in Bali! It was a bit of a secret concern for me when we first got together that Marc would never be able to come and enjoy Bali the way I do. The idea of big waves and reef breaks worried him. Back then, what I considered to be a two to three foot wave scared him shit-less. Yet today at Legian beach he was ruling the lineup in five foot surf! It was so cool watching his beautiful relaxed style as he cruised, cross-stepping up and down his board on the green-blue face of the wave. He still hasn't made it to the nose, but I reckon it won't be long now.

Where ever Marc paddled today the waves just seemed to come to him. He would jump off one wave, paddle out in the rip and sit up on his board for ten seconds' rest before the next set wave would peak up just where he was. In stoked amazement, he would paddle two strokes into the next long ride all the way to the sand. As I saw him disappearing off down the line while yet another set wave landed on my head, we were both grinning from ear to ear. To see it working for him, to see him loving Bali so much when he was once so apprehensive about coming here, means the world to me.

9/10/02 Legian Inn

We ended up at the bloody Sari Club again last night. We both got way too drunk and spent the night at opposite ends of the club. He wants his space and I got mine. I hate the effect alcohol has on us. We had an argument and went back to Legian Inn early.

We talked it over and I went to bed, but Marc couldn't sleep and was acting strangely. He paced up and down the room saying he felt terrible, and when he finally lay down he insisted on leaving the light on all night, which he has never done before. It was as if he was scared of the dark. When I finally dropped off, my dreams were fitful and restless. One particular dream was surreal but strangely vivid:

I fell from a height, having jumped off a high building as if I was escaping from something. I landed hard on my feet and hands, jumped up and started running, only to stop in the middle of a black and nightmarish street frozen with fear. There were burning car wrecks on the road and it seemed like everything in front of me was on fire. Many people were watching from the darkness behind me as buildings burned.

My first instinct was to wonder where Marc was, so I turned and ran through crowds of people calling out his name and putting my hand on people's shoulders to turn them around, until finally I found him. As he turned to face me, his eyes lit up and we embraced in the middle of the street. As smoke swirled around us it was hard to breath. We held each other tight and I whispered to Marc in fear: 'Something horrible is going on. *What* has happened?'

'It's okay babe. I don't know what's happened, but we're okay, and we're together, and that's the most important thing. I'm right here,' Marc whispered in my ear as he held me tight.

I sat bolt upright gasping for air, awaking to find Marc on the other end of the bed. His arms were pulled around his knees as he rocked nervously back and forth, back and forth. The room was filled with the grey light of dawn and it was clear that he hadn't slept. He looked terrible. I must have looked pretty spun-out myself as he asked me what was wrong. As I rubbed the sleep from my eyes I told him that I'd just had the most screwed up dream.

'There were fires. Something awful had happened, like we were in a war zone or something.' I shrugged. 'I dunno... It was awful, but just a stupid dream,' I replied, shaking off the feeling of foreboding.

'What's up with you?' I took my turn to ask.

'I- I can't sleep. I feel disturbed!'

'*Disturbed*. What's up, babe?' He looked really out of sorts. This whole thing was right out of character.

'Well, you know that normally in life you kinda have an idea about the future, and when you think about it you can sorta see images of what you plan to do?'

'Uh, yeah, I guess I can.' I thought about the plans we'd made for when we got back to Australia, and how Andy had emailed to say he'd found a beautiful place for us to live. I imagined the green trees and the wooden verandah he'd described.

'Well, I can't. Not anymore. There's nothing there.' He looked at me with wild eyes. 'It's scaring me.'

I didn't know what to say to comfort him.

'I'm sure it's nothing. You're just apprehensive about our move back out to Oz. We'll be fine. We can make it this time!' I reached over to cuddle him.

'I hope you're right babe. I really hope you're right,' he replied, closing his eyes and shaking his head, before resting it on my shoulder.

It's a weird world. We are living a pretty good life, with fun surf again today, but still I'm feeling pissed off and un-easy… Out in the courtyard I was speaking with Oka this morning, who was telling me that locals are not allowed in the Sari Club at all, and have to pay a lot of money (in local terms) to go into Paddy's. I had no idea. How have I not realised this injustice before? Imagine if that happened in Cornwall – that locals were banned from the Driftwood while tourists could go in. It would never happen so how has it been able to happen here? Oka often goes out with Australian or European friends and they can't go to the Sari Club as he isn't allowed in. It seems crazy. There is so much inequality even on our doorstep, and I really have lost the desire to ever go back to that place.

10/10/02 Legian Inn

Before dinner we watched some snippets of news with Oka and Mama. Afghanistan ... they've bombed the shit out of it, innocents died (probably a lot more than on September 11th) and Bush is harping on about *his* God, using religion as an excuse to kill. Bin Laden goes on about a holy war. Now John Howard has joined the 'War on terror'. Afghanistan is not guilty of the Twin Towers attack, so why are they bombing it? They don't even know Bin Laden is there! They just want to be seen to be doing something about it, I guess. When are they going to look in the mirror at their own part in the problem?

After dinner we went back to Legian Inn early and stayed up late into the night talking. I'm amazed at how much I learned about Marc last night that I didn't even know. He told me the detailed story of leaving his wife. It hurts him still to remember how miserable he was, how much time he wasted trying to make it work. How she constricted him and finally turned on him. I found a part of myself I had not shown to Marc before, and we talked about things we had never delved into. I feel as if we've finally weeded out the seeds of doubt and faced together the pain of the summer just gone. Now is our time for coming together again.

12/10/02 On the road

There are lush green rice paddies on both sides of the road as we drive southwards down the Balinese west coast. Our skin is encrusted with salt and our hair still damp from the surf. Marc's driving so I'll try to write even though the Suzuki Jiminy we hired gets the speed wobbles at 60km/h. Wow, what an insane time we've had! We're now on our way back to Kuta as the American crew will be back from the boat trip by now, and it's *Saturday night* in Bali! They should be amped up after seven nights on a boat.

Last night we stayed at the most amazing hotel ever. We stumbled upon the place looking for a surf spot called Medewi. We took a little random rocky lane through the trees, past some tiny villages to a hotel nestled alone on an empty beach, hidden between the banana palms. It had to be five star, with the reception opening up through large marble pillars.

'*The Puri Dajuma,*' read Marc from freshly carved stonework. We knew full well it was out of our price range but we had a look around anyway out of pure curiosity. I wanted to take a look down on the reef behind the hotel to see if there was any potential for waves. Sri, a friendly local girl with long black hair swishing down her back, guided us through the hotel asking us questions about our trip. Speaking in clear English, she told us that the hotel had opened only a few weeks before.

'Where are you from?' she asked as we walked through carefully manicured gardens on winding cobbled paths.

'Cornwall and Australia,' said Marc.

'Oh, Australia! My sister lives there. I want to visit her. Do you know Brisbane?' As we chatted away merrily she showed us the beautifully crafted, Balinese-style bungalows, the air rich with the smell of sea spray and frangipani flowers. The restaurant, spa and bar were all elegant Balinese constructions, open to the air and centered around a large pool. The restaurant was full of staff who were having an English lesson, and Sri introduced us to them as they waved coyly. I exchanged a few words of English, then a little bit of Balinese and they giggled and smiled widely:

'Ah! You speak bahasa Balinese!' said Sri, also smiling. 'You can get a good discount!' She grinned cheekily. Marc and I turned to look at each other: could we really entertain the idea of staying *here*?

We heard the rumble of breaking waves and looked out to the blue ocean just beyond the reef. The courtyard was set just above the reef with the calm shimmering surface of the pool flush with white polished marble tiles. Sri stopped and gave us her best Balinese smile as she held her palms up to our surroundings, both welcoming us and inviting us to stay.

'What do you think?' I whispered to Marc as Sri waited patiently.

'It's pretty pricey,' Marc whispered back.

'Well, why don't we head up to Medewi, check the waves and see what the places are like up there?' I said.

'Ok, let's take a look, maybe we can come back,' said Marc. Sri gave us a nod of understanding, waving as we drove away. We drove back through the rocky lanes to find Medewi point just ten minutes up the coast. The waves were crumbling and uninviting, with a couple of local grommets having a grovel. There was an old hotel right on the point, so we took a look around at the old musty rooms with squat toilets and peeling paint walls (which is my normal travelling style). We took one look and climbed back in the car, heading back to the hidden hotel on the reef.

Between the marble arches, Sri waited to welcome us.

'You've come back!' she said happily. Marc nodded to Sri with a smile as she handed him the keys to our Bungalow. When Marc held the door open for me, we laughed with glee. The room was all white, with a white bed-spread, white marble floors and white tiles in the en-suite. We jumped on to the bed sitting to face each other cross-legged, smiling as we sipped our complimentary cocktails, the clink of our glasses echoing off the walls.

We walked down to the reef to wander among the rock pools in the evening light. As far as the eye could see the tropical coastline disappeared into a gentle haze as black sands met jungle. A small headland of black rock jutted out to the south. The waves looked good, with a couple of different reef breaks peeling left and right, but we didn't feel like surfing. Instead we were content to explore the labyrinth of rock pools, picking up seaweed necklaces and watching little crabs scuttle about the rocks. There was a curious sculpture on the reef of a Balinese boat filled with soldiers; an ominous statue to be found in such a place.

'I wonder what it represents…' I said. It looked old, and some of the soldiers were amputees, their legs and arms having long-since eroded away. It gave me the shudders.

We returned to our room, put on a couple of long white robes and went back down to the pool where we jumped in the cool water, playing about. One of the other guests walked past, laughing at us trying to take underwater photos of ourselves. We slipped into the oval marble spa. Sri brought us an Arak Madu (Arak and honey) each and we sat squeezing lime into our drinks and looking out over the sunset with a frangipani placed behind each ear.

'Does it get any better than this?' asked Marc.

'I dunno. Who knows what wonders await?' I mused. I threw my arms around his neck as he pulled me closer and we kissed slowly. Every sense was dancing in delight.

Down in the candle-lit restaurant, reggae music played. We ordered our favourite meals and managed to forget that we were just another pair of poor surfer bums for just one night. It feels amazing to be together like this, like falling in love again only better this time because we've travelled a rocky road and come out the other side. We know each other so well and we know that we love each other. Waking up this morning together in the fresh flower-scented air, we could hear birds chirping and the rumble of waves on the reef. It feels like the beauty is only just beginning: we made our mistakes and we are certainly not making the same ones twice. I'm finally starting to understand and come to terms with Marc's weirdness over the summer. I can now see how needy I became, and how I pushed him away.

As we lay together this morning, I could feel the tenderness has returned. He is the man I truly love. We've just had an amazing surf at a break I'd never been to before. We'd said goodbye to our friends at the hotel and were driving southwards down the main road, looking for a surf spot I'd heard a rumour of, somewhere along that way. I spotted an old sign with a wave painted on it next to a little half hidden dirt track, so we turned off the main road towards the coast. The narrow track got narrower and bumpier with coconuts all over the road as the Jiminy pushed through the greenery. It looked as if we were going to end up right on the sand when the road swung a hard right and the bushes opened up to a wide grassy area. Massive coconut palms stretched out hundreds of metres above us.

As we pulled up, two guys were sat on the grass next to a tiny hut right on the sand. They smiled a greeting, waved and called out 'Hi' before the car had even stopped. Our attention was taken quickly by the surf, which looked awesome, peaking left and right with no one out. We jumped out and walked over to the guys. One of them had short fair hair and a strong surfer frame.

'Hey guys, welcome to paradise! My name's Jules,' said one, a local, shaking our hands and introducing us to his Aussie mates and Ketut, who ran the joint.

'Yeah, just paddle out in that rip over there; the right peak is the best today,' he said. I was surprised at their friendliness – surfers are not usually too open about the surf. It was Marc's first time on a sizey reef break, but he paddled straight out next to me without a whinge or even a blink. We took it in turns to paddle into the green bowly waves. Marc took the steep drop easily and carved some wide turns, walking up towards the nose. He came off one wave whooping at the top of his lungs.

'What happened?' I asked him as he paddled back out.

'I hung ten!' he said excitedly.

'Ten toes on the nose? Perfect!' I cheered. Marc's surfing is taking off now! After hours of perfection we finally caught a wave in, but had to wait for Ketut to finish his surf before we could get some noodles (which was all he served), and boy were we hungry! The Aussies came in too, exhausted from days of surfing perfect waves. As we ate our spicy mie goreng, the muscliest guy I'd ever seen suddenly appeared over the grassy slope behind the beach. He was dragging a log, which he threw down to join a pile of wood on the sand.

'Oh yeah, we're having a party down here tonight. Why don't you stay?' asked Jules, looking at us both. I envisaged the evening of guitars and singing by the crackling fire on the ocean's edge. That has to be one of my favourite things to do.

'I'd love to! What do you reckon Marc?'

He also nodded. 'Where can we stay?'

Under Jules' direction we walked up and over the slope to find some huts hidden behind the hill. The lady showed us round the basic but beautiful open huts with mossie nets draped over neat beds. We both liked it, so we decided to stay.

'Damn it,' I said, with a sudden realisation.

'What?' asked Marc.

'We went and booked into Cempaka to make sure we had a room when the boys got back…'

'Ah shit, can you ring them up?' said Marc.

'Sure.' I turned to the Balinese lady:

'Is there any way I could use your phone? I'm happy to pay.'

'Sure, *no* worry,' she replied smiling, showing me to their office. The only problem was that I couldn't remember Cempaka's bloody phone number. I tried to ring directory enquiries but couldn't get through. We decided we may as well head back to see the boys as it would be good to catch up with them anyway. Marc was keen to dance in the bright lights of Kuta.

'Maybe we can come back here tomorrow?' suggested Marc

Back to the hot sweaty accommodation I am far more accustomed to: the fan revolves slowly and noisily overhead with the thick heat immediately destroying the freshness of the shower I just had with a new peel of sweat… but I love it! No sooner had we arrived than we rushed straight out for dinner with the American crew. We walked over to Warung Linggar, open to the street with its little woven lampshades hanging down low from the ceiling above tightly packed wooden tables. Bobby and Marc were sat opposite with Bobby's friend Blaine. I shared a tuna pizza with a pretty blonde English girl called Mel who happens to be leaving tomorrow, and so is keen to go dancing...

Bobby isn't as keen to party as I might have hoped. He said he'd have a shower and think about it. Unfortunately, the man with a rubber arm, Timbo, is still on Lembongan 'till tomorrow. Of course, Marc still wants to go out, with the new excuse to celebrate Mel's last night, as he never turns down a chance to party. I can hear the guitar starting up outside on the terrace. My cold Bintang's waiting. I'd better put down this journal and get amongst it.

Chapter 8

Hell in Paradise

WE DID ALL we set out to do, singing the evening into the night. Marc played all his old favourites, from Tom Petty's 'It's Good to be King' and Buddy Holly's 'Peggy Sue' (because it annoys me).

Marc sat on the terrace with the green guitar on his lap, the mozzie coil winding a whisp of smoke around his ankles. He was wearing the orange shorts (again) and one of his favourite t-shirts, sipping on a large Bintang.

'Bintang!' He tried a poor imitation of a Balinese accent as he held up his beer in a salute to us all before taking a swig (he sounded more like Speedy Gonzales). Bobby cackled as he wandered up to join us, reading Marc's shirt out loud:

'Your village called, they want their idiot back ... Nice.' He nodded his head with a smile, swigging on his own Bintang.

Marc glanced at me with a cheeky smile as he started to sing:

'Oh Peggy Sue, Peggy Sue, pretty, pretty, pretty, Peggy Sue...'

'Rah! I hate this song!' I protested, laughing, before singing along. Next, as Marc started to sing our song I closed my eyes and listened to his beautiful voice.

'Sail away with me honey, I put my heart in your hands, Sail away with me honey, now...' I still loved to hear that song, especially hearing it this time. I was dreaming of the fresh start we were set to make in Australia, now that we'd grown together through our hard times.

I wasn't originally going to go out. Bobby and the boys had decided they were getting up at five for an early Sunday surf sesh at Canggu, and I committed to the early start, *but* Mel and Marc were so keen to party, being Saturday night n' all. I went into our room and closed the swing-doors, considering my choices. It made sense to leave them to it and get an early night... However, it was only a few days ago I'd said how I would love to have a girlfriend to party with. I rifled through my bag and picked out some funky suede shorts with tassles down the sides that had been my birthday present from Marc, pulling on a black singlet my sister Mellie had sent from Italy, together making up my 'Lara Croft' outfit. When I pushed open the green doors dressed in my party gear both Mel and Marc cheered.

'Lara can do both! Why not dance and then surf too?' I joked. I swapped my hard boots for sandals because of the heat – which was lucky for Mel. I kept treading on her poor flip-flopped feet as we walked down the busy lane to the Sari Club. A group of children followed us, holding up their open palms with tired, wide, dark chocolate stares. I had long-since learned to ignore them. You give to one and ten more will follow you the whole way, calling out to you: 'Please miss, *one* dollar…'

Mel wanted to go to Paddy's but it was dead so we ended up at Sari, of course. It was about 10:30 and I decided that I'd be out of there by 11 and tucked up in bed after a dance or two. A line of sellers bustled outside offering cigarettes, marijuana and jiggy-jig to all those entering and leaving the club. We wound our way past the bouncers in to the busy club, hanging by the bar as the dance floor filled up. Marc and I shared a jungle juice, which was so strong I couldn't even drink it.

You never know quite what you're getting with jungle juice. The mix is never the same and as arak is cheaper than orange juice, well, that's just asking for trouble! I decided to do the familiar rounds, popping across the road to Paddy's a couple of times looking for Blaine. Of course, then a song came on that I *had* to dance to and I dragged everybody onto the dance floor.

My memory is hazy. There was laughter and silly moves and cheesy tunes and… just… general silliness. There was a group of very young, very pretty girls with their hair in tiny braids (a sure sign of it being their first trip to Bali). A pissed-up Aussie guy with no shirt and lots of mates cleared the dance floor to make way for a running jump onto his belly, sliding through the spilt beer to the whooping amusement of his mates. It was pretty funny but the floor was filthy. I thought he was lucky there was no broken glass on the ground. I looked around, remembering what Oka had told me, noticing that the only Balinese in there were working behind the bar. I couldn't really relax into it, but I've always tried to make the most of every situation. I love the saying: 'go hard, or go home.' My personal variation was 'dance hard, don't drink, then go home and get up for the early surf.'

I got into the groove, dancing to all sorts of cheesy shit, shaking our heads in mock embarrassment as we grooved to 'I'm too sexy'. The Sari, at the very least, is a place where you just dance as if no one is watching. As I lost myself in the groove, I recalled years of Bali trips between Paddy's and the Sari.

'Do you believe in life after love,' started to play; a song Marc particularly hated, as he couldn't stand Cher's electronic voice. He raised his eyebrows at me as it came on, and indicated his jungle juice was getting low, shaking the bottle.

'Sorry guys, I have some pride!' he laughed as he walked off, disappearing into the crowd.

'See you in a bit!' I chirped and turned to face Mel. It was my Bali song, but of course Marc didn't know that. When that song first came out I was eighteen years old and out at Paddy's on my first solo trip. I'd recently experienced my first break-up back in Australia, so I'd danced harder than ever to that tune when it came on. Whenever it played, in whatever country I happened to be in, it always took me straight back to that filthy, steamy dance floor in Bali, under the flashing lights, watching Cher on the big screen. They played it every night in those bars. I always chuckled at how the music lineup would never change each night: the same stuck record in both bars. You could hear *Land Down Under* downstairs at Paddy's and wander straight across the road to Sari only to hear it again. By the time you'd had a dance and wandered back to Paddy's to see who you could find, it'd be playing again, upstairs this time.

From the speakers, 'Murder on the Dance Floor' started to play. I looked around, wondering where Marc was, as we loved to play up to that song. I couldn't see him, but instead two drunk and creepy young guys sidled up to Mel and I. We tried the subtle brush-off manoeuvres but they didn't work, and neither did the turned back, or even the elbow in the ribs. I was thinking how ironic the song was, as I wanted to kill these guys! Rather than resorting to stomping on their toes, I danced Mel away to the back of the dance floor, further from Marc who was watching us from the sunken bar at the front of the club. We now danced in the corner of the L-shaped bar which spanned two sides of the dance floor. The Balinese guy behind the bar was swaying to the music as he served the next jungle juice with a smile.

We reveled in our new space with plenty of room to boogie. 'Without Me,' came on. As we watched Eminem dressed as a superhero flashing on the big screens above the dance floor there was a loud bang over the music. It was not a familiar sound, but no one paid much attention until the electricity flashed off, and we stopped for a moment, glancing about as the music took a few seconds to come back on. I tried hard to place the sound. Was it a shotgun? Surely, not in Bali. Was it a party banger? A car back-firing?

Maybe … must be, surely. A chill rippled up my spine. The air in the club shifted as if a wave had passed through. The lights flashed on and off. Something wasn't right, but despite the uneasy feeling in my gut I took the decision to go and check it out when the song was finished. If anything *was* wrong there was no point in running straight into it, I thought.

That momentary decision was to save my life. Unbeknown to me, the inquisitive Marc wandered towards the door, jungle juice in hand.

The music started playing again, the screens flicked back on. On the chorus the beat was thick and Mel and I were getting low, bending our knees, wiggling our hips as we grinned at each other.

'Last song for me,' I muttered below the music, as I imagined the crystal sunrise waves at Canggu.

The noise which came next I will never forget. It was an empty sound that did not resonate. It was a thud, like the slam of a car door but multiplied to a volume I simply cannot describe.

The sound is all around, blasting through my ears, my body, my soul. It feels like someone has burst a hot air balloon on my face. My hair is streaming and my ears are screaming.

All the air in the club is sucked out, replaced with a gust of hot pressure, which picks up the dancers and the whole club like a dumping wave or an angry child throwing dolls and pencils with a frustrated shriek. I'm being hit by the biggest, most powerful wave I have ever known, except it is hot.

In slow motion I see the club around me explode, ribbons of fire tearing through poles and people flying through the air as my mind captures this moment in a three dimensional photo. As time slows I am picked up and suspended in mid-air, twisting to face down as I slam to the ground.

As everything hits the floor I find myself in eerie blackness. I lay amongst the rubble as I feel the roof collapsing around me, stopping close above my head. After the impact comes the silence, stretching out for an eternity as the music of the Sari Club stops forever. No one knows what has happened, and the living have not yet realised they can still scream.

And as I lie here I can feel the pressure of rubble on my back. Am I still alive? I think that this silence is the end, and that this simply must be my time. I feel a peace floating over me, and I can accept that what will be, will be.

But, *oh no*, all the things I want to do but can never do, all my dreams, hopes … gone.

Another voice comes into my mind screaming a clear message: 'NO!' As I snap from my daze, the voice speaks clearly: 'What are you thinking? Get out of here, NOW!'

Right. If there is any way out of here I am going to find it. I try to move my aching body, and to my amazement it responds: I throw off the wood, tiles and whatever is covering me to crawl out on my belly. Thank God. In the darkness I can hear Mels' voice close by.

'Hanabeth! Are you OK?'

'Yes! Are you?'

'Yes. Don't panic, we'll get out of here,'

Where is Marc? He'd been standing too far away to know now. We're on our hands and knees with several others crawling under the collapsed roof, away from the amber glow at the front of the club. If we don't move quickly we might be trampled as there are people moving behind us too, pushing in the darkness. A hot and putrid stench burns at my mouth and nostrils and thick smoke is gathering all around as we crawl, trapped under the rubble. I notice the ground is soft, and in horror realise that there are people under my feet, alive or dead I do not know, but I can't stop. I kick off my sandals … I know that every split second counts. I can see the ominous amber glow growing from the front of the club. I know I'm very far from safety, and every sense is on overdrive as I feel my way through. We find a hole in the collapsed roof through which we can see the stars, and people immediately start to surge upwards onto the roof. I stretch my hands up the rubble to pull myself through, pushed from behind. Everything is hot to touch, like the stones of a fireplace. The part of my mind still stuck in the world of thirty seconds ago curses at the loss of a good pair of shoes.

'Oh, it's okay, I'll probably be able to come and pick them up tomorrow,' I think momentarily, just as another voice in my head screams: 'What!! Fucking shoes, what about Marc?' It is like my brain has split in two as it struggles to comprehend this reality. My heart thuds as I think of Marc. There is no way back, but, *where* is he?

'Marc!' I scream out loud but no answer comes. Again I can hear Mel's sweet reassuring tone:

'Don't panic, keep calm.'

But the girl behind her screams: 'Run! RUN!' I think that is a more appropriate approach right now.

I find myself on the thatch of the roof. Around me I see the fallen roof broken up into so many segments and different levels, trying to make sense between what I can see now and what was supposed to be here before. Everywhere I look I see patches of flames in the straw lighting up silhouettes of those coming out behind me ... *Where* is Marc? No, I decide, it's hopeless. To turn back will be death. N*ow* is the time to run, *now is* the time to panic. My blood runs cold as I see that we are amongst the kindling of a massive bonfire, well on its way to catching alight. I can't see Marc so I can only hope beyond hope that he is close behind, or is finding his own way out (of *course* he is).

I use both hands and feet to scramble up the roof like a monkey, moving as fast as I can as the adrenalin surges into my veins, jumping across gaps between the roofs. The fire is getting louder and the flames are starting to create a dull roar as they advance across (and under) the roof. I try to push through what seems like a window between tiers of the roof, but a man and I jam shoulders and as we both pull back to surge forwards, it happens again, yet neither can fit through unless we take our turn. We pause:

'After you,' I say.

'No, after you,' he pushes me through and follows. We jump down to the ground, safe and free. On second thoughts, *no*, we are not. As I look up my heart sinks and then rises to my dry mouth in fear. In front of me rises a towering wall, and I realise that we are still in the club. I don't remember this wall. Where am I? My eyes scan up and down the tall, grey wall to see no steps, no way forwards, no way out. To my right are flickering flames and to my left a couple of guys are boosting girls up the wall. Should I ask for help? No (that voice again): I am able bodied, I'll let them help others and themselves. There must be a way to do this by myself. Searching the darkness, the only light is the flickering, growing wall of flames behind me, casting my tiny shadow on the grey wall. The thick power lines that had been hung along the front of the club now lay severed and hanging down the wall. Could they be live? I hope not, but what is my alternative? Without hesitating I grab the rubber casing firmly and run up the wall, hauling myself about four metres up in seconds.

'Argh!' I yell as I rip some skin off my knee while pulling myself onto the top of the wall. It could be worse. The rough top of the brick wall is only four inches wide, and on the other side, far below there is nothing but rubble. ... It's funny, I can't remember there being a building site here. It's a short distance to crawl along to where the flimsy framework of a roof remains, as long as I don't look down. The roof is little stronger than a pile of matchsticks, so I choose my steps carefully as each hand and foot finds its place to manoeuvre slowly, following behind a Balinese man.

As I reach the other side, my heart sinks again as I am met by a large drop, the size of the one I've just climbed. I can see piles of debris; broken tiles, wood, shrapnel and glass littering the ground. People are down there staring up at us as we appear over the rooftop. One man yells out to me:

'I'll catch you, you can jump!' (Bless him) I yell back for him to help others first, as I would probably just injure him if I land on him, anyway. I'm able bodied enough. I climb carefully down to the edge and ease myself down until I am hanging from my hands. I can only pray as I release my grip, dropping like a stone.

I feel the full impact of the drop, with my knees bent as I fall back on to my hands. I turn to look back over the roof I've climbed over. There aren't many people coming over the same way; I think I must have been one of the first out of there. Maybe I can help others down, but my size and height make it seem pointless. I'll just hurt myself. I scan the people on the roof, searching for Marc coming out behind me. Maybe he got out first? I run across the road, stopping in the middle, taking in the scene of fire and panic around me. The whole street seems to be in flames. The sound of a car horn stuck down makes an eerie background noise to the cries of human panic and suffering. I feel a huge rush of blood to my head as I remember this place. I've been here before, in the dream of four nights ago. This was the exact same scene. What *has* happened?

The gravity of what is occurring finally hits me as I see a body being dragged away from the flames by a Balinese man; it is the body of a young man, with only skin flapping where a skull used to be. My heart goes cold as I take in the orange shorts he is wearing. The blood rushes to my head and my heart thumps in my chest. But no, these are plain shorts and it is the body of a teenager. I see the pale skin and freckles, maybe European. They are orange boardshorts: not Marc's, not Marc, yet still that image burns in my brain. I can't see Marc around me so I run between the burning cars to try to get to the south side of the street towards the front of the club, and maybe back in to get Marc. If not, I want to get to Cempaka to see whether Marc has gone there, and to see Bobby and Blaine. The flames are thick, so I brace myself to try to run along the narrow blackened pavement, between burning buildings and cars. As I run forwards I can see several blood splattered bodies on the pavement to my right. There is someone moving in the orange glow of the flames. I crouch down to see a young male, alive.

'Oh my god,' I mutter, as I crouch down and grab his hand. 'Can you move?' I shout above the roar of the flames and the chaos.

'No, I can't,' he replies in an Aussie accent. He can't be more than eighteen years old. I glance up at the flames ripping from the car only a few feet away. I try to haul him up, but he is much bigger than me. I have to shout: 'Look, I don't give a damn if your legs are broken, you have to get up now otherwise you're not going to make it! I can't carry you but I'll help you all I can.' Thank God, he is trying to get to his feet. It's all I need, so I use his own momentum to pull him up, holding on to his left hand and locking it over my left shoulder. It's wet, and as I look down I notice it is completely red, sodden with blood. I feel sick – I'm not good with blood at the best of times. I put my right arm round

144

his waist, taking on as much of his weight as I can. When we are clear of the flames two men approach us to help the young man, freeing me from his weight. I immediately turn a full circle: Where is Marc? Where is he? I can't stop so I just keep on running and searching. Finally I find Mel standing wide-eyed on the corner of the alleyway. We rush towards each other and embrace. Mel speaks first:

'I'm so glad you're okay. Where's Marc?'

'I don't know Mel, I didn't see him come out. I can't find him.' I can hear the fear and thickness in my own words, and they scare me.

'It was a car bomb. They fucking bombed us,' Mel says.

'No way!' I reply firmly, shaking my head. There's no way there could be a car bomb here. 'It must have been an accident …' My words seem naïve, even stupid.

'Maybe it was a gas explosion?' I mutter. I cannot believe this is a human, deliberate action. Who would, who could, do this *on purpose*? We look back towards the club we were dancing in five minutes before. Red and orange flames stretch up high above the roofs, eating into the blackness. Suddenly it dawns on me, and my internal organs feel like exploding from my body.

'Oh my God, there's people still in there. No-one's coming out! Mel, are there people still in there?' I ask hysterically.

'No,' she says, 'I think everybody got out.' Is she just trying to calm me?

'Look at the people around! They didn't, Mel! We have to go back!' I start to run back towards the front of the club, my heart ready to burst out of my chest. I feel a hand reach out as Mel grabs my arm and pulls me back, stopping me from running back into the flames. But I have to get back. I have to do everything I can to get those people out. I struggle with Mel, trying to pull away, but she cries out:

'Hanabeth, NO! There are still petrol tanks and gas bottles that are yet to explode. Stop! You will get yourself killed. Marc will be fine. He'll be looking for you on the other side. It's not as bad as it seems.' As she locks me in her arms her tone is soothing, and she is speaking all the words I want to hear, but I know she is only trying to comfort me. As much as I want to, I just can't believe her. My body goes limp as powerlessness engulfs me. I stare at the enormous tower of flames and something in my heart turns cold and still. This time I speak in a quiet tone, half calm yet half a whimper.

'He's dead, Mel. He's gone, I can feel it.' Somehow I feel quite sure and I speak as if it were a matter of fact.

'Don't be silly. Don't give up yet! Think how many places he could be. He will turn up soon,' she reasons. I want nothing more than to believe her, and have no intention to stop looking, but I have a deadly feeling deep down that is difficult to ignore. How can you love someone that much and be that close to them and not know the moment they leave this planet?

Suddenly there is renewed panic – everyone around us starts to scream, running up the street, sprinting away from the flames. They are yelling something about another bomb. Maybe another petrol tank has exploded. Before I know it I too am running amongst all the others, sprinting up the street until eventually I come to a halt, as many sprint on. It seems a little crazy, and I don't know what started it. So I wait for a very short while before I jog back down the blackened road, calling out to the injured lying on the side of the street.

'I know CPR, can I help anyone?' My voice rings out with a question I quickly realise is ridiculous. It's hardly any help to those lying under the column of smoke feeling their skin burn as their lifeblood runs from them. What can I do? How can I help? How can I find Marc?

'We need water!' someone yells, as they attend to an injured man lying on a makeshift stretcher.

'Hanabeth, we have to get water.' It's Mels' voice. She grabs my hand and leads me across the street. At the mention of water I become aware that my mouth is very, very dry, and a choking, thick horrid flavour sticks inside my mouth. I have never known such thirst. We duck into a restaurant and walk up to the bar, pleading for water. Between us we have no money. Mine was in my 'handbag' (Marcs' pocket). The barmaid kindly hands over two small bottles of water. In our frantic thirst we forget what the water is for as we rip off the lids and throw our heads back, glugging down the life-giving liquid. Suddenly it occurs to me, there must be a mirror here. I pull Mel into the bathroom where there is a little light and we can see ourselves in the mirror for the first time. I take a step back in shock to see my face smeared with blood, my whole body grey-black from the smoke and the explosion. Our hair is thick with dust, dirt and blood. I turn around on the balls of my feet, examining my limbs, my skin, checking myself for injury. I know enough about the effects of shock to know that either of us could be running around with serious injuries. Mel turns on the tap and we rub at the blood, finding nothing more than mere scratches underneath. The blood is not from our veins. We stare at each other, astonished that we are unharmed. But still, Mel is unsure. She holds out her arms:

'My arms hurt. Could you look at them?' I examine the backs of her arms where she has indicated, but can see nothing. I feel the bones in her arm gently.

'You seem okay, Mel. Everything seems intact.' In my shock and naivety I do not stop to consider the possibility of burns.

We shout our thanks to the bar staff as we rush outside back into the chaos. Mel takes the water to the young man and once more every scrap of my energy is focused on finding Marc. I cross the street, pushing through the crowd, turning people around, looking for his face somewhere amongst the chaos. The silly boy (it's almost funny) had dyed his hair jet black a few days before, to cover the three faded blue spots left over from his mushroom outfit for the SAS Ball. Looking for his dark skin, I turn around a hundred men that could be him, only to reveal unfamiliar Balinese faces. Never before have I longed so much to see his wide grin, his gangly arms, feel his warm embrace. Once again I remember my dream, as I had pushed through the crowds searching the faces … and, yes, in the dream I'd found him. This renews my hope to keep going. I must be running around in circles because I keep finding the same young man lying on a stretcher made from a large shop sign. His jet black hair is sticky with blood. How many times already have I stopped in my tracks to stare at his face? I gently stroke his head and tell him he is just fine, although I doubt it.

'I don't want to die here. Please don't let me die,' he begs of me and Mel, who is staying by his side holding his hand. Her soothing voice and kind words must mean the world to this young man.

'It's okay darling, you are going to be just fine. Don't you worry,' I hear her say, over and over.

My heart breaks a thousand times tonight. I want to stay with him, but I must find Marc. I cross the street again to climb up on a white jeep, standing on tiptoes trying to see past the flames to the south side of the Sari Club. There lies my hope that Marc is alive, and I hear myself screaming his name:

'MARC!! MARC!!' I cry out over and over, until my voice is hoarse, then I just keep screaming his name anyway. If only a weak reply were to meet me through the chaos. Again I recollect my dream from the week before and the moment when I found Marc in the darkness, but this is beyond any nightmare that has ever crept into my sleep. I run back to Mel still screaming his name, frantic now.

'Have you seen Marc? Where is he? Mel, I have to find him one way or another.' She stares at me through scared but kind eyes.

'Marc will be fine, darlin',' she reassures me, as she looks down at my feet. 'Hanabeth! You are standing on broken glass!' I look down at the floor to see the remains of a shop window piled under my bare feet. Suddenly I become aware of a dull ache in the soles of my feet. I grab my ankle and balance on one leg, pulling several thick shards from deep in my flesh. Once I'm free of the glass I am running again, weaving through the crowd, this time more conscious of trying to avoid the worst of the glass.

Time is passing, so surreal and twisted that I have no idea of the speed or the sequence of its passing. We have helped to move some injured people into taxis. After an agonising wait, fire engines and ambulances start to turn up. I'm guessing it must be more than forty minutes since the explosion. This is too little too late. I've been running in circles in the dark for such a long time. It is Mel who finally instigates the move.

'Hanabeth, my arms are really sore.' She now has my full attention and I examine her upper arms under the fire light, seeing bubbles starting to form on her skin.

'Oh shit.' Finally, I realise my stupidity in not recognising that she has been burnt. Someone produces a wet rag which we press on the burns. I look around, scanning the crowd again. I have to have just one more try.

'Just wait thirty seconds. Wait right here.' I run off once more to look through the crowd one last time. I slow to a walk, coming to a stop back next to Mel, finally deciding that my chances of finding him at the hospital are greater by this point. I grab Mel and virtually pounce on a motorcyclist.

'Will you please take us to the hospital?' Suddenly my voice is clear and urgent. The Balinese teenager nods and we jump on the back of his bike, Mel in front of me so I can keep holding the wet rag on the back of her arms and shoulders. A man comes up to take a photo of us and we scream at him in anger.

'How dare you take photos at a time like this! Fuck off!' As the camera flashes I give the photographer the finger and we speed off through the seething crowd, away from the flames into the black night.

Chapter 9

Goodbye Innocence

W E CHUGGED AWAY from the smoke and the fire and straight into the fumes and traffic on the back streets of Kuta, only to find that the road was blocked. I was horrified to realise that most of the traffic blocking the road was made up of taxi drivers sitting alone in their cabs. Looking back at the ambulances struggling to get through, I banged on a window of one of the cabs and gestured for him to pull over. If only they would pull up onto the curb, the ambulances could get through with the injured and the dying, but they didn't, and the gridlock continued. At least on the bike we could weave between the cars and up over the pavement.

I became aware of a pain deep in my lower back. The initial shock must have been wearing off and I worried about what damage may have happened to my spine. Things were getting hazy and I seemed to be losing control. Somehow we were directed to get off the bike and into a four-wheel drive driven by a German wearing a smart white shirt with a black flowered pattern. There were several other survivors huddled in the back and I lay on the floor, trying to rest my throbbing lower spine. The journey seemed to take forever. The Germans told us they were on their way to the hospital to look for a couple of girls that they were to meet at the Sari, when they saw the blast from a hundred metres up the street. Somebody handed me a mobile phone and I instantly dialed the number for Cempaka: 754 744. I even knew the area code. I had a rush of blood to my head as it dawned on me that if I had remembered that number earlier that day, I would be far from here sitting by a campfire singing songs with Marc.

The phone barely rang before Bobby answered. 'H! You're alive!' he cried, 'are you ok?' I heard the relief in his voice.

'Yes, Bobby, I'm okay,' I replied. 'Is Marc there?' There was a long pause before Bobby spoke again.

'No, H. I haven't seen him. I mean, I don't think I've seen him.'

'What do you mean? Where have you been?'

'I've been looking for you, H. Blaine and I got thrown off our beds when the bomb went off.'

'Bomb? Are you sure?'

'H, I'm pretty damn sure. We leapt up and went running straight down Poppy's 2 to Legian Street and ran straight into the thick of it. H, it's bad, really bad. We saw a lot of injured people and a lot of death. I nearly lost Blaine but he's okay now. That's another story. We just got back here hoping to find you. Thank God you called. I thought I'd lost you, H. How did you get out?' The German looked back at me, gesturing that I should wrap it up.

'Over the side. I was really lucky I think. Mel's with me, but she's burned her arms. We're on the way to…?' I looked up at the German who responded

'Sanglah.'

I spoke back into the phone: 'Sanglah. The biggest hospital, apparently. Hopefully we can find Marc there, looking for us.'

'Okay H, we'll be here. Call me if you need anything. I can come and pick you up, whatever you need,'

'Thanks Bobby. Hey, and love to Blaine,'

'Sure H.'

The hospital was seething with people everywhere. A crowd of Balinese clustered outside the main entrance. Whether they were there to look for loved ones or just to stare I couldn't tell. A sick feeling in my stomach told me it was mostly the latter. One by one, a procession of cars, taxis, Jiminys and bikes pulled up, delivering the gravely injured who were grabbed by a group of men and hauled into the hospital building as rapidly as possible. Mel sat on a bench as I stood beside her still trying to keep my spine straight. I knew it could easily be nothing, but my lifeguard training warned me to be cautious of spinal pain. As the blood-splattered tourists and locals passed by, I stared at the frangipani tree just metres away, my eyes fixated on the beautiful pattern of white and yellow flowers amongst the green, illuminated by the harsh fluorescent lights of the hospital building.

I glanced back to check the next casualty who passed me by: not Marc. It was a young man being carried on a wooden board that looked like a sign torn down from a shop. I wondered if this was the young man Mel had been looking after. I remembered the car had left with him close to an hour ago: surely it could not be the same person? I watched his black, spiky, blood-soaked hair, his badly burnt skin starting to peel already. I think it *was* the same young man.

'Mel, let's go in. Hopefully we can find him inside.' I paused. 'Hopefully we can find him looking for us.' Mel looked back at me. Already I could see in her eyes that she was less certain than she had been.

'I'm sure he is.' She sounded weak and drained. 'I need some painkillers.'

We walked into the corridor, following dirty footprints and droplets of blood scattered across the floor. I grabbed Mel's hand. We turned a corner and found a nurse.

'Please, do you have any painkillers?' She looked at us blankly. 'Aspirin?' I asked. She shook her head sadly. 'Sorry, no have. Finish.' I pointed at the bubbles on Mel's arms, some of them now an inch across. The nurse just sighed and apologised as she shuffled off. By this time I was desperate to use the toilet and as I closed the door of the tiny room my heart sank. Just seeing the filthy state of this basic facility in the hospital reminded me of my Mother's words: '*Don't ever* end up in the hospitals in Bali. Do *anything* to avoid it.' Now I could see why – this hospital was in way over its head. As Mel and I walked through the wards looking for Marc it seemed as if the hospital was never ending, just ward after ward of old metal-framed beds lining up as far as the eye could see, like a scene from a war movie. Every bed held its own set of horrors as women, men and children lay screaming out in pain. Mel and I looked at each other in shame. We were fine. We didn't need any pain killers. It was all I could do to approach people and try to give them some comfort. Just to speak with them and have a stranger hold their hand might help them in some way.

Mel and I walked into the emergency ward, a small room surrounded with beds on all sides. In a series of cubicles at one end lay a row of people. I looked at the grey skin of a Balinese security guard lying there as I walked past. He was dead. The nurse pulled the green curtain across and rushed to the next bed. In the centre of the room were mobile beds pulled together in an uneven row. A slim blonde-haired woman lay screaming as blood flowed from her arm socket. Another man with both legs missing lay shuddering as great waves of shock ripped through his body. He too was screaming in fear, pain and confusion. Chaos was all around us. The woman's screams ceased as she passed out, whether simply from pain or from blood-loss I did not know. A wet sensation crept up from my feet and I looked down to realise in horror that I was standing in a rising tide of blood. Widening my gaze I could see the whole floor of the emergency room was covered in blood an inch deep. I never had allowed myself to watch films this violent, yet this was real. I dug my nail into my arm and winced: yes, this was real.

Beside me stood a man in a white shirt with black flowers. He had kept popping up over the night. I assumed he was a nurse and asked him whether he had seen Marc. He looked at me in confusion as I started to describe Marc. 'I drove you here,' he said in a thick German accent. That simple mistake scared me – making me realise the thin grip I had on reality. By now we had been in the hospital for what felt like hours. We had visited every ward two or three times and had run back out to watch the bodies and the injured come in, with no sign of Marc. At no point had he come running around a corner to embrace me with a relieved look on his face. 'There are more hospitals,' the German spoke. 'Perhaps your boyfriend is there. We will look for our friends. Would you like to come with us?'

'Yes please,' I replied. We drove to three, four, five or six more hospitals, medical rooms and surgeries. I simply don't know how many. At each place all we saw were more destroyed human bodies. When eventually we found ourselves back at Sanglah, Mel turned to me and spoke: 'Hanabeth, we can't do this all night. We are just getting in the way.' She brushed back her blonde hair, grey with ash. 'Marc could be anywhere.' I realised she was right; this endless running was futile. The German turned to us and gave us an opportunity to escape. 'It's impossible to get into Kuta. The whole area is blocked off,' he said. 'We have a place at Canggu. You can come and wash off the blood, get a few hours of rest, and we can come back in the morning when things have settled down.'

Leaving the hospital felt like such a betrayal to Marc but I looked at Mel, who was exhausted and the pain was taking its toll on her. All I could picture at that point was Marc, bloodied and torn, heavily injured and reaching out a hand, screaming for my name in the darkness. I had to push the image aside as I nodded my head.

'Thank you, but I *have* to be back here at dawn,' I spoke in a whisper. 'Can we not get back to Kuta?' I wanted desperately to see Bobby and Blaine.

'There is no way through. We'll be lucky to get through to Canggu.' Reluctantly, I agreed and so we travelled away from the corridors of hell, northwards through dirty winding streets, trying to ignore the orange glow on the horizon behind us.

We drove upon a levee along a narrow road between what I knew to be rice paddies, although of course it was pitch black, maybe four in the morning. The lane ended at a large building with white marble walls towering above the arched entrance. We walked inside to find a black stone swimming pool filled with lilies, sparkling lights highlighting the surface of the water from within. The courtyard was carefully manicured and the pool was surrounded with palms and fragrant frangipani trees. A colourful bird called out to us from behind the bars of a small wooden cage. A large ornate table was filled with the remains of a banquet; stuffed ducks and colourful rice was laid out between piles of fruit atop banana leaves. We were ushered by another German man in his late sixties to sit in comfortable chairs by the pool where we were handed drinks. I tried a few sips of vodka and orange, but it tasted horrific. I placed it down on a low table carved from ebony. 'Could I just have water, please?' It was a confusing contrast from where we had been just minutes before. Reality felt as if it were bucking and warping. The young Balinese boy who I had realised was the playboy of the old German sat down beside him, staring at us. 'Would you like to use the phone?' he offered.

'Oh yes, please, please. I need to call my parents...' I thought for a moment. I couldn't possibly call Carole and Ray yet, not until I knew either way. By now my thinking had changed. Seeing all those poor people and the horrific injuries they had sustained had made me wish for only one of two options: 1. Marc had been looking for me and we had somehow missed each other (perhaps he was back with Bobby right now?)... Somehow I was finding this harder to believe. The second option was that Marc was dead and had been killed instantly, with no pain or realisation. It felt strange to be wishing for this but, knowing Marc, anything in between would destroy his spirit and I couldn't bear to think of him with limbs missing as I had seen so many others that night. Where was he? He had to be *somewhere*, alive or dead. I prayed that he was not lost to the flames.

When I was handed a mobile phone I dialed the number to where I knew my parents would be sleeping peacefully in Byron Bay. My father answered the phone. It was so good to hear his sleepy voice, a thread of reality.

'Dad. There's been a bomb in Bali. I'm okay but Marc's missing.'

'What do you mean a bomb?' His voice became clear and urgent very quickly as he asked a succession of questions. I tried to answer them as calmly as I could, describing briefly the events of the evening. Once again, the older German said something about his phone bill and I cut the call short so Mel could call her own family in London.

Next, we showered in a huge bathroom of polished stone. I watched the soot, blood and filth run from my black top as I tried to wring it out under the running water. I left the suede shorts aside. As I picked them up, at first I was surprised at how clean they were, until I turned them around to see their back splattered with dried liquid of dark red.

We were handed some men's t-shirts and boxer shorts. Mel rubbed her hair with a thick towel as I climbed into a large bed. I helped her to press ice-soaked towels onto her burns, the altered sense of reality enlarged by the grandiose nature of our surroundings.

I lay there for perhaps an hour, staring out the window at the stars. As the first light of dawn paled the sky, I jumped up and walked outside, my bare feet pitter-pattering on the polished floors. I walked into one of the rooms to ask for a lift back to Kuta. The man grunted and turned over in his bed. I walked into another room only to be surprised by the same response. 'I'm sorry, I know it's early but I simply *have* to get back to Kuta. I have to find Marc and *cannot* rest until I do!' Eventually one of them spoke to me grumpily:

'You can call a taxi, there's a phone at the restaurant just a couple of hundred metres away.' I backed out of the room: surely they could not be so heartless as to leave us stranded here? Without a pause I pushed open the heavy front door and marched outside. I looked across the rice paddies to the restaurant, a lone wooden building upon the levee. I ran to the front door to find that, of course, it was closed. A young Balinese girl stood outside and watched me run towards her. I asked her desperately:

'Kuta! I have to get to Kuta!' She shrugged but pointed over my shoulder to a white Suzuki Jiminy, thirty metres away. A tall thin man stood by its open door and stepped towards me as I approached.

'Please, I have to get to Kuta right away.' He took one look at the urgency on my face, and perhaps also at my strange clothes, and replied immediately.

'Of course, please get in. My name is Christian.' As he held out his hand I noticed his accent also had a German lilt. I could see that his eyes were kind and shone with compassion. I nearly cried in relief as I grasped his hand briefly.

'Thank you so much! I just have to get my girlfriend. She's in there.' I pointed at the white marble villa.

'Okay,' he replied. 'I'll wait here.' I ran along the levee and stopped suddenly. The light was growing stronger, filling in the colours of the green rice paddies and banana trees. The coolness of the morning breeze brought with it the sounds of the jungle close by, the chorus of cicadas and the birds singing out all around me. I could hear the waves crashing on the reef not far away. The sky was vivid pink and orange and without warning the sun appeared through the clouds on the horizon, scattering gold across the sky and land as the world awoke into all the glory of its colour and life. I heard myself speaking out loud:

'How can this *be*? How can I be surrounded by such calm, such beauty and perfection so soon after such horror, pain and fear?' I watched the sun rise through the multi-coloured clouds. It had been my plan to be at Canggu for dawn...This is where I was supposed to be.

Hearing Mel approach, I turned to greet her. We both paused for a moment looking at the sunrise in disbelief. I turned and pointed silently to the horizon behind her, narrowing my eyes as my head dropped slightly. We could still see the fires of the Sari Club and Paddy's smoldering far away in Kuta, the black smoke billowing into the sky in a thick column.

'I've found us a lift back to Kuta.' I pointed to Christian who was driving towards us. He pulled up and opened the door for us.

'It can't be long now until I find Marc,' I thought as I climbed in.

Christian drove carefully through the chaotic streets, still very busy for that time of morning. He said he'd heard the news and it seemed fairly certain that it had been a car bomb. He told us that he was there to help us in any way he could. At a traffic light, I looked up to see a young Indonesian man stopped on his motorbike right next to us, pointing through the window at the burns on Mel's arms. In horror I realised that he was laughing at us. I pulled Mel towards me, away from him. Why would a Balinese man be happy about this? *Why* would he take pleasure in our misery? Confused, we drove on to Cempaka where Bobby was waiting outside. He flung his arms around us. Blaine came up and did the same.

'Have you seen Marc?' I asked immediately. Bobby shook his head sadly.

'You're really okay?' He spun me round slowly, looking me up and down, checking for hidden injury. 'Fuck, it's a miracle, H. How *did* you get out of there? Where were you when it went off?'

'Right in the middle of the Sari,' I replied. 'I don't know exactly where Marc was. Where's Timbo?'

'He's still on Lembongan. Back soon. Right, we've got to find Marc.' He stepped back and looked at us again in our attire of blue boxer shorts and mens T-shirts. 'Maybe you should change your clothes. And H, if you have a photo of Marc could you grab it please? It might help someone tell us where he is if they recognise him.'

'Sure.' I walked through the office past a succession of sympathetic eyes belonging to the Balinese guys who worked there. I tried to smile but failed, just looking back down at the red brick pathway as it wound through the courtyard. I trudged past a long row of rooms, under papaya, mango and hibiscus trees to the far end where my room was situated. Incense was burning everywhere and special offerings were scattered outside every room. This must only be a hundred metres from the back of *the club*, I thought to myself. Tiles from the roof were scattered on the ground and the dark green swing doors of our room had been blasted open wide.

I stood at the edge of the patio. Everything was just as we had left it only eight hours before. The guitar was just where Marc had carefully placed it, next to his half-drunk Bintang. I walked into the room to see where I'd dumped the boots I'd discarded just before I ran out the door. The ceiling had partially imploded so everything was covered in dust and soot. I grabbed some clothes and, searching through our bags, found a photo of Marc and I at the SAS ball. I quickly left the room, closing the doors behind me.

Once again we were back in the hell of Sanglah, but thankfully we had shoes on this time and Bobby and Christian were by our side. The majority of the panic had subsided but the pain, the anguish and the fear was clearly apparent in the faces we passed by in the hospital beds. There was a subdued calmness in the hospital staff who moved as quickly as they could from bed to bed. Many doctors and healthcare workers who had been on holiday had joined the Balinese in the care of the injured. I held up the picture of Marc to many faces but all remained blank and heads shook slowly, sadly, helplessly. I was just another one of many marching the corridors desperately clutching a photo. Eventually I could look no more at the wounded. All I could look at were the blackened and bandaged feet at the end of each bed, knowing I would instantly recognise Marc's long, tanned feet. I must admit that by now I was only half hoping. All I really wanted was to see him walk around the corner.

We went back into the emergency room. The floor was mostly white once more, but great piles of blood soaked material had been pushed to one side. A small group of good-looking blokes were getting their cuts and burns attended to as I walked in.

'Smile,' said a young Aussie bloke with the physique of a footy player. I realised they were probably from some sort of team. 'It can't be that bad,' he said.

'I don't know how bad it is yet,' I said through gritted teeth. 'How dare you!' I turned and marched out to where Bobby and Christian were talking quietly together. The poor guy was only trying to make light of a dire situation but I was angry all the same. I found out later they'd lost half of their team in the Sari Club.

Bobby took the photo and disappeared with Christian for a time. With every second that slowly ticked by the torture of not knowing was taking its toll. Exhausted, I waited with Mel by the entrance, sitting on an unused stretcher. Next to us, a long list of names of the living, injured and missing was being written up on a wall. Crowds of people thronged around reading the names as I searched for Marc, constantly scanning the sea of faces that passed me by. I saw a head of black spiky hair moving slightly above the crowd and I stood up instantly, only to sit back down as the Balinese face appeared, walking past us into the hospital.

After what felt like an eternity later, Bobby and Christian returned with a solemn expression. As Bobby sat down beside us he turned to look at me:

'H, we've been to the morgue. We've found someone wearing orange shorts but we're not sure it's Marc.' My heart thudded slowly as the world turned to liquid around me. 'We're not sure. We're gonna need a detailed description of what he was wearing.' I described his shorts in detail, along with his watch, jewelry and shirt.

'Does he still have his head? Was it blown off?' I asked.

'If it's him, yes, he does. We just want to be sure.'

'Why don't I come with you?' I asked.

'H, it's pretty bad in there. Maybe its better if you don't. But it's up to you. Come walk up with us.'

Mel and I followed Bobby and Christian through endless winding corridors to the far end of the hospital. We came to a stop outside a separate building with ventilation along the top of the walls.

'Just bring me a square of material from the shorts and I can tell you,' I said. They went back in one, maybe two, maybe three more times, and on the last time Mel went in as well. I watched the door close as they disappeared inside the morgue. I stood waiting outside as the heat of the day descended. As usual the bush around me was teeming with life, and I could hear the sound of small birds tweeting. I looked over to see their blue tails shining as they danced in the morning sun. It was as if I was watching the world through a veil. The pain, the sick anticipation and the fear were about to change. Soon I would know, either way.

When I look back now I wish so much that I had gone in there myself, but for some reason I just didn't. My reasoning was that I didn't want to remember him that way. But in the weeks, months and years that followed, I imagined his horrific injuries so many times that perhaps I may as well have gone in myself to identify him. The intention of my friends was to spare me the images that will probably haunt them for a lifetime. They paid a high price for me.

Finally, the door opened and Mel, Christian and Bobby came to stand in front of me. Bobby gave a slow sad nod as he spoke.

'It's Marc, H. We're certain. It's him. I'm so sorry, H.' The liquid veil swirled around my head, my heart splitting in my chest, my mind spinning as I collapsed into a heap.

'How did he die?' I asked breathlessly.

'He was killed instantly and he wasn't burnt. Something hot and heavy must have landed on his head.' Somebody reached out to touch my shoulder, but there was little consolation for me at that moment. Marc was dead. My love, my soul mate, with all his perfections and imperfections alike, would never be here to hold my hand again. He could not console me. Finally the breath sucked into my lungs as loud sobs resonated up and down the corridor. It felt like cheating for me to breathe, for my heart to beat, for my eyes to blink, but at least, finally, the waiting game was over. After a few minutes I stood up straight.

'Who hates us so much? Why do they hate us so much? Why this? Why does it have to come to this? Why us? We were just... dancing.'

'I don't know, H,' was Bobby's reply.

'Somebody really hates us,' was Mel's reply.

'The truth will come out eventually,' said Christian.

'I have to tell Carole and Ray,' I said bluntly. 'I can't bear that they could find out from somebody else. I have to tell his parents.'

'Now?' It was Christian who spoke. I looked up at him, thinking of the blissful sleep Carole and Ray would be having at that moment, ignorant of the tsunami that was set to rip through their world. Right at that moment they were ignorant of the fire, the flames, the hell that had stripped this world of their son, and the children and mothers, brothers and fathers of so many more. But we had already told the official and the British Embassy was due to be notified. I imagined a stiff official making the call to Cornwall... No, I couldn't allow that.

'As soon as I can,' I said firmly. 'They have to hear it from me, not from anyone else.'

The phone rang for several seconds, before I heard Ray's sleepy voice:

'Hello?'

'Ray, it's Hanabeth,'

'Hello Kid, is everything alright?' My voice somehow remained calm, yet inside I was panicking. *How* do you deliver news like this? H*ow*?

'I've got some awful news. There's been a bomb in Bali, in a nightclub. Ray, we were in there... Ray, Marc's dead.' I heard a muffled sound on the other end of the phone, then a thud as Ray's knees hit the kitchen floor, and then he was screaming:

'NO! NO! NO!' I could hear the sobs and the pain beginning, tearing an everlasting hole in their lives. I heard Carole's shrieks in the background as the news passed quickly on. At that moment, I knew that no matter what happened in life, it could not ever get any worse than this.

Chapter 10

The Heart Keeps Beating

THE FIRST THING I did was light a Sampoerna. Sitting on the tiles outside the green swing doors, I inhaled the sweet clove cigarette as the smoke wound its way into my lungs. The deep breaths somehow slowed me, calmed me. I struggled to my feet in the thick humid air grasping the photo of Marc, stepping into our room to find everything just as we'd left it. Tears flowed continuously down my face. I picked up the open tub of Marc's Dax hair wax. As I inhaled the familiar smell I noticed that it was filled with dust from the collapsed roof. I walked into the bathroom and stared at the pair of toothbrushes sitting in a cup on the red ceramic sink. I slumped on the bed and stared across the room to a large dusty gold and red ornamental fan that poorly covered the mold and peeling paint on the opposite wall. My gaze dropped to Marc's longboard leaning against the bed. I folded over in grief as the world spun around me, loud sobs echoing off the walls.

What the fuck was I to do with his board? What was I to do with his bags, his clothes, *all* of his things? When the hell was Marc going to walk through the door and apologise for making a really bad joke? What the hell was I supposed to do, to feel, to be? How could life possibly *continue* from this point? I rang Mum. She'd been on the phone to the Australian Embassy for hours and hadn't been able to get through. Finally she'd rung the British Embassy and so a slight, fair-haired, middle-aged woman came by to pick up Marc's passport and ask me some questions as I sat chain-smoking Sampoernas. I think I was smoking mostly to remind me to breathe. She said that emergency flights out of Bali were being arranged. I said they needed to evacuate the injured first, but of course I wanted to leave as soon as possible. As she left she said she didn't know how long it would take, but would try her best.

Everywhere I walked I had four personal bodyguards with me. We went over to Warung Linggar for some food, and to catch up with each other. Mel had already flown out of Bali and was one of the first to return to England, while Christian stayed close by to keep a concerned eye on me. Timbo was finally back from Lembongan with another American friend, innocent of the horrors we'd seen. This was just as well as Bobby, who had been my rock through the whole ordeal, was understandably starting to show some cracks. The mild-mannered Blaine had been through his own nightmare as he'd worked with Bobby to pull people out. Thankfully Blaine, who had planned to come and meet us at the Sari Club, had laid down for a moment and fell straight to sleep, only to be thrown right off his bed when the bomb went off. They'd all come running out of their rooms, and Bobby had known instantly, shouting: 'They've bombed the Sari!'

Immediately they ran down Poppy's 2 to help with the rescue effort. Bobby spoke of one tall fair-haired man who had been sitting on the curb outside the Sari. He seemed calm except that the lower half of his right leg was perpendicular to his body, resting sideways on the ground beside him. Blaine spoke of the helplessness of choosing who to help first. They'd tried to pull as many people out as they could, working with about ten others at the front entrance right where the car bomb had gone off. Some had run right into the flames to grasp at hot sheets of corrugated tin to release men and women trapped underneath, and Bobby himself had run in several times to pull people out. At one time Blaine had put his hand right through a body as he'd tried to pick it up.

In the midst of it all, Blaine, who was diabetic, had gone critically hypoglycemic and had drifted off in a daze – not a good state to be wandering around in at a bombsite. Bobby had lost him for a while but thankfully found him in time to give him a blast of sugary coke to bring him back. It turned out that the wall I'd scaled was the way that only the relatively uninjured had been able to escape. All the rest had to make it through the hell of the furnace at the front of the building. I'd had it easy, it seems.

I stared at the menu, blurry through my constant tears. There was no way I could eat anything.

'Try, H. *Please* try to get something down,' said Bobby, as he looked at me, concerned.

'Yeah come on Hb, at least try some white rice,' said Timbo. I ordered some rice and a mixed juice, tidak gula (no sugar). The juice was easy enough to suck through the straw, but this was worse than when everything tasted of dried Weetabix. I tried to control the wetness streaming from my eyes and nose, slowly making my way through all the tissues from the holder on the table. I'd been crying for over a day now. After we'd sat trying to eat for a while, Bobby finally looked up at me and spoke.

'H. I've got to say something important. I can't even imagine how you're feeling right now, and I understand you gotta cry, but you've also got to realise that we don't know that we're out of this yet. We just don't know. Maybe just try to keep your wits about you until you're out of here, H. Then you can let it go.' All the boys looked at me through concerned eyes. Christian nodded, now linked to us forever through the terrible experiences of the previous twenty-four hours.

'Hb, we just want you to be safe,' said Timbo, and the others nodded in agreement. 'And we're right here with you. We're not going to leave your side until you get on that plane.' I nodded and stood up. 'Thanks guys,' I said, taking a deep breath and wiping the tears away. 'You're totally right, this might not be over yet.' I left the table to go into the bathroom. Staring at the mirror I struggled to block the stream of tears, but they slowed and eventually stopped. As the steamy mist cleared I was shocked to see my own face. I looked like a different girl – more a woman now. I could see in my own eyes that something was missing, gone forever. I soon realised what it was: my innocence was gone. How *could* I ever be the same?

Later that day, the Indonesian President Megawati came to visit the site. As Indonesia's first female president, she was a moderate Muslim who was unpopular with the more extreme factions of the Indonesian archipelago. The military lined Jalan Legian along with thousands of Balinese, ex-pats and tourists alike. Wearing a turquoise t-shirt, a red skirt and my customary rice-farmer's straw cone-hat, I wandered towards the black pit where the Sari Club had been. I weaved my way silently through the crowd, oblivious to the thousands milling around me. I wanted to see what was left of the club and make some sort of sense of where I had been the night before. Somehow, it was as if I was invisible. I walked past the crowds of staring tourists, past the police, past the military and past the officials until I was looking straight into the crater where the car bomb had exploded. The hole in the road was probably a metre and a half deep, now filled with water from the fire fighters.

Before me rested the thin tatters of what had been a hideous, yet iconic Bali nightclub. The steel innards of the blasted structure drooped like wilted flowers. As far as I could see, every tile on the roof had been blown off, leaving only naked wooden frames. Every window was smashed. The thick black snake-like power lines lay severed and limp. The club was almost leveled, with only piles of unrecognisable charred material amongst the corrugated tin that had supported the straw roofs. Several car wrecks stood where they had burned, their drivers long-reduced to cinder and dust. All around me on the ground I could see thongs (flip flops) and sandals of all shapes and sizes. I felt sick to my stomach: there were hundreds of shoes scattered across the road. The sickness rose in my stomach as I noticed a pair much smaller than my own feet.

I flashed back to the night before when we had wandered in there, to the crowd of Indonesians surrounding the entrance asking for money from the drunk tourists, the children stretching out their palms. I could only assume that several of the begging children had been hurt or killed. I thought of the mothers who carried a baby with them as they begged. I flashed back to the moment before the bomb had gone off: the stupid dancing to the cheesy music under orange and red flashing lights, the ignorance and innocence of the dancing tourists.

As I stared at the blackened rubble I contemplated what all this meant. *Who* had done this and *why*? Why? What was there to gain from blood and destruction? Immediately I thought of the wars across the world, particularly Afghanistan where I knew bombs ripped bodies limb from limb on a day to day basis. In front of me I had seen the effects of just one bomb. How could anyone *ever* do this to another human being? I stood there humbled at my own pain and loss in light of how many other people in other countries were exposed to horrors such as this *every day*. As pictures of this daily violence reach us in the comfort of our couches, where we are free to safely glance at our television sets, sometimes we may experience a fleeting pang of remorse before we change the channel or turn our attention back to our dinner.

Staring into the crater, I thought back to Gran's descriptions of the Second World War, and what they had been through as they fought for 'peace and freedom'. *The war to end all wars?* Something did not ring true because the violence was not over, and now it had struck at us, right here on the Island of the Gods midway through a pop song. Marc, who seldom paid any attention to politics, had now become an unwitting pawn in a game of violence that somehow felt global. I didn't understand it yet, but I sure as hell was going to try to make some sort of sense of all of this.

A journalist approached and asked if I had known anyone in there, and when I told her that I had, I was surprised to find the cameras immediately turned on me. I simply told her my story, how I had escaped, and how Marc had not. I told her the facts, but I also asked her, 'Why? Why do they hate us this much?' They took a photo. An Australian news crew came over and filmed me telling my story and then I spoke with others. After a couple more, I felt exhausted so I pushed my way back through the crowd, unable to comprehend nor escape this strange reality I had found myself in.

The next morning I woke up to a call from Dad.

'You're all over the news,' he said. 'I think you're in the paper. What were you wearing?' Strange question. Still, I thought back to my interviews the day before.

'Umm, a turquoise t-shirt and a red skirt. Why?'

'Oh,' he replied. There was a pause as I heard the crinkling of a newspaper.

'I'm sure it's you. It looks like you. Did a man help you out of the Sari Club?'

'No. What *is it*, Dad?'

'It's the whole front page of The Australian. There's a man carrying a girl out of that shit hole the Sari Club. She looks like you. It's *got* to be you!' Suddenly I remembered the young man I'd picked up right after the blast. Did someone really take a picture of *that*?

'No! Dad, it's the other way around. I helped someone out. There was a man on the ground when I was looking for Marc so I picked him up. He was right next to a burning car... In the bomb I was wearing leather shorts and a black singlet.'

As Dad replied I could hear the shakiness in his voice. 'Yes, it's definitely your watch and your ring. It's you. It's quite a picture, Hanabeth.' I heard more rustling paper. 'There's an interview with you on page two as well, but there's no connection made with the photograph on the front.' After hanging up the receiver I looked around at the dusty reception of the losman. It was time to get out of here.

My flight back to Australia was brought forwards a few days. As I drove towards the airport through the narrow lanes of Poppy's 2 and along Jalan Legian, it was clear that the tourists had already left. In fact everybody was gone.

It was just three days since the blast and Kuta was a ghost town, with broken windows kilometres away from what they were now calling Ground Zero (a very American term). On the plane I was moved into business class and was a wreck of my former self. I sat down next to a large blonde woman, my ears still ringing with tinnitus from the blast. I was so scared to fly, so scared of the noise of the plane as it took off, so scared that my life could end at any moment. The blonde woman let me hold her hand until we made it into the air. Who had I become, holding onto the hand of a stranger?

After landing in Brisbane we were allowed to exit via a back door to avoid the press. As soon as we got outside I smoked another Sampoerna, the very habit I'd helped Marc to give up. Dad, who had never seen me smoking before, eyed me in despair. I knew how much he hated smoking, but it was all I had to steady me right then. I inhaled deeply. Mum was there too and it was a strange emotion, hugging her. There was still a residue of unresolved issues which had now been overlayed by some very mixed up feelings. I was going to need her now.

A day or so after my return, we arranged to hold a small dawn ceremony at Dolphins Beach, not far from my parent's house. The wind was belting across the beach as we struggled to carry Marc's huge longboard and numerous bunches of flowers down to the shore. It was a brief ceremony, but many friends turned up and sat in a circle around Marc's board. Peter Jensen and his family came down from Mount Tamborine to join all our friends, and Tommy of course, but

I can't remember much more. We passed around spliffs and a bottle of tequila as some of us said a few brief words in Marc's honour. Then we waded out together with his board covered with flowers. We pushed it over the waves until the flowers had washed away, and then a few of us took it in turns to catch a wave on his board. Lee dove under and came up shrieking in excitement:

'You can hear the whales! Put your head under. Listen!' he cried. Quickly, we also dove under and, sure enough, you could hear the whales singing clearly. We floated for some time, taking deep breaths and diving down for as long as we could. Eventually we walked back to shore. Dan turned around and pointed back out to where we had been swimming.

'Look!' he said. And sure enough, there was one lone dolphin out there surfing alone, cruising across the green face, jumping off the back of the wave with a splash.

Since Bobby's warning, my eyes were dry most of the time, yet still the world had a misty dream-like quality as I drifted around as if made of vapor. With the constant stream of phone calls and visitors, both from the press and my friends, I didn't even have time to have a shower or clean my teeth. Well, I kind of forgot. Normal human functions like getting dressed and eating, any sort of personal maintenance, were forgotten completely. I was back in Australia for about a week, I think. I remember those days as a hectic blur where I was mainly stuck in my parents' house, with Tommy marching up and down trying to organise the family and the press. He was halfway through building Mum and

Dad's house next door and was now doing his best to keep everyone above water, while not letting the media get on top of me. Dad simply wandered around worrying, in an utterly dazed state. Mother regularly handed me bits of fruit and food, which would often be put down and forgotten, or guzzled by one of my hungry helpers.

I have an almost comic memory of Andy and Lee trying in vain to pull me away from the chaos and madness of my parents' house, to get me to the beach for a surf or a walk. I could not be alone at all so they both camped on the floor of my room. Lee was normally cheerful and smiling and now he was devoting much of his time to trying to make me smile. Andy usually had something interesting and deep to say about the environment or some new project, but now he was just trying to get me away from the media.

'Just grab your bikini and jump in the car," Andy whispered sideways to me. 'Lee will get the engine running and we can make a quick getaway before any more of these bloodsucking weasels get hold of you and you're stuck here all day.' I was observing the conversation taking place between Tommy and Patick Aventurier, a tall dark-haired French photographer from Paris Match, who'd flown from Paris just to take a photograph of me, which I couldn't quite get my head around. Apparently, Paris Match was kind of a big deal over there. Tommy thought to ask whether they'd care to pay me for an interview.

'Of course,' he answered immediately in a thick French accent. 'We could start with something in the region of, say, ten thousand dollars.' I looked up at Tommy with vague interest. Money meant nothing to me, but he had a stronger grasp on reality and knew it would help them to finish the house and help me to get through the next few months. I shrugged my shoulders as if to say, '*Whatever; I trust you to work it out.*' Besides, I needed some money to pay for my flight back to Cornwall to be with Carole and Ray. Patrick asked whether he could come and take some photos of me at the beach. Completely naïve and always keen for some surfing shots, I said: 'Sure, I don't care.'

It was a quick turnaround. I jumped in for a surf in a small, choppy, warm ocean at Byron Bay and then finished the interview, leaving myself half an hour to pack my bags to leave for an indefinite stay in England. I was heading from the Byron spring to the Cornish winter. This pendulum swing was the wrong way round, I thought to myself as I boarded the plane. I had no idea what I was heading in to. Andy came with me, following a last minute decision to have a close Byron friend come to the funeral. And besides, I could not fly alone.

Lian took some time off work to pick me up from the airport while Andy headed north to visit his mother. For some strange reason we were worried how it might look, my arriving with another man in the village (a strange thing to worry about, in retrospect). Lian dropped me off at the Doble home. We stopped off at Chapel Porth and walked over the windy cliff towards the engine house at Wheal Coates. She listened intently as I told her the story of the couple of weeks since I'd seen her, which felt more like a thousand years. Wherever we were, I watched her worried eyes flick my way every so often. After a few days she had to go back to work so Laurs took over staying with me up in 'The Playroom,' which had been renovated since we had grown up. The piles of toys and fancy dress had been re-placed with polished wooden floors, three double beds and a couple of massive black bean-bags. There was a tiny grey kitten called Tess who hung out with me up there. Jenny now insisted that we call it 'The Studio', but old habits die hard and to us kids it would always be The Playroom. I stood on one of the beds and stuck my head out of one of the many skylights in the sloped roof, looking out over the bare trees to the grey wintry ocean below.

The Dobles lent me a little white car. I drove across Corn-wall to see Carole and Ray, stopping at the petrol station on the way. The pump was playing up and kept clicking off. Confused, I kept trying to make it work, clicking it on and off and rattling it about. I'm not quite sure how long it took before I noticed that I'd been pouring petrol onto the ground. It had been overflowing from the tank, which of course had been filled up by the Dobles before it was given to me. I stared at the puddle on the ground in disbelief. What planet was I *on*?

Carole opened the door of their little cottage, eyes red-raw with tears, stains on her usually spotless white t-shirt. Ray walked out to greet me, engulfing me in a tight embrace. Already they both looked older, greyer, with laughter lines worn into new patterns by grief. It was hard to tell who was crying harder. It was as if our hearts were breaking all over again as we saw the pain in each other's eyes. We sat down opposite each other in their little lounge-room. The flickering fire provided neither warmth nor solace to our frozen hearts. It was good to be together to share our grief but still, whatever could we say? I quickly realised there was a whole other level of this for them. Although it was unimaginable at the time, perhaps one day I could find another man but they could never have another son. Thirty years of love and care had evaporated in the scorching moment the Sari Club was blasted to bones and dust. We sat blinking, holding our teacups and looking at each other, each forcing a smile.

I woke each morning with a jolt. '*Where is Marc?*' was my first thought, and the answer was always the same. He was not here or anywhere: he was dead. Every day it was the same, my first reality check of each new dawn. I avoided going into the newsagents but when I went around to friends' houses I saw pictures of myself in the papers lying around. I found it rather odd to see a photograph of Marc and I on page three of the Sun, usually reserved for topless girls. It was so surreal. I drew a cartoon picture in my diary of myself with my hair puffed up and a shocked expression as if I had just stuck my finger in a light socket. That was how my mind felt most of the time. In the picture I stood frozen in the middle of a blackened street, flames and burning buildings all around me. It was a memory from my nightmare, and from reality.

Until the funeral, I couldn't even consider grieving properly or trying to do anything with my life. I started to drink a lot. It helped me to fall asleep and stopped me from thinking too much. My memories of the days, weeks and months that followed became a blur.

Sitting with the Dobles, or next to Gran's little fire, I poked the food around on my plate. Everything I normally loved tasted uninteresting and dry. For a while I could not even swallow a mouthful of Gran's pasties. As usual, I found my solace in the ocean, standing by the wintry shore watching the seething water. A friend leant me a winter wetsuit and I just spent my days surfing, smoking pot and drinking myself into a stupor before passing out at some late hour. I went through a stage of waking up at 3.30 or 4 am with a red wine headache, when I would lie in bed writing, or go out walking on the cliffs in the grey dawn.

I was hovering in limbo, neither moving forwards nor backwards, in complete shock. Each day was a constant case of sink or swim, and I discovered that I survived pretty well under those circumstances. I was determined not to let those terrorists destroy me too – enough had been lost already. I often heard people say how strong I was, as my eyes were now dry most of the time, and in public I was mostly cheerful, or drunk, or both.

The media interest slowed down for a short while, although I agreed to an article with *Marie Claire* – hoping to get my message of peace across to readers. I did not like how so many bomb survivors were calling out for retribution in the media. It was as if their grief was being misused. There was growing talk of 'weapons of mass destruction' in Iraq, and I feared a war.

The photographer from *Marie Claire* was due in half an hour, and my skin was coloured white to green. Laurs was in the toilet with me holding my hair back and making reassuring noises as I threw up red wine-flavoured vomit. Matt and another couple of our mates had brought their DJ decks over and we'd played up to his house music in The Studio until the small hours. I'd passed out at some point about a foot away from the thumping speakers with an empty bottle of red wine lying on the floor by my bed, red-wine stains on my lips.

The photographer wanted to get some shots of the locality. I took him to my favourite spot on the cliff at Wheal Coates so he could take some shots with the blustery ocean behind me, propping myself up against the beautiful old engine house. As I focused on staying upright, I could hear the waves beating at the tall, dark, wintery cliffs below me, throwing sea spray high into the air.

I learned to love Sundays, because that was when everybody went down to the Driftwood for the best roast dinner money could buy. Pissed up on cider, I would stumble back up Rocky Lane to the Doble house to find the yummiest home-made roast waiting for me on the big kitchen table, followed by a delicious apple and blackberry crumble, also made lovingly by Jenny. Despite my usually tiny appetite, on Sundays it was hard not to eat well.

Every day I explored the cliff-tops. Sometimes I wore a raincoat and walked with my eyes half-closed to the drizzle. Other days the sun shone on the cold crisp land, and I could see all of Cornwall stretched out from the top of the Beacon. It was at the top of these cliffs that the raves had been held over summer, but summer was over now. I turned up my collar to the winds ripping up and over the cliffs, sweeping through my hair. Regarding the rocks and boiling ocean far below, I shoved my hands deep into my pockets and trudged back towards the village, turning up the side of the narrow valley, alongside a bubbling stream, up past a salmon farm with a big water wheel. The path wound through low forests and glades, past yet more old ruins, to the tiny Jericho Cottage where my Mum and Dad's best friend Dave Lee lived alone. I popped in for a cup of tea on my way past. Dave always looked slightly scruffy, with a tattered blue and white sailor's top to accompany his short beard and grey hair. His eyes flicked down at the lino floor as he stammered:

'Uh, uh, I'm so sorry this has happened to you, Hanabeth … So sorry.' No one knew what to say, and I didn't know what they could say anyway. Everyone I spoke to was so sad, so sorry for me. They would often apologise to me for the way things turned out, although they had played no part in it. The look in their eyes broke my heart every time. I could see all of their pain as if looking into a mirror.

On another footpath southwards from the village, I walked past the defiant silhouette of Wheal Coates in a cool glowing sunset. I made my way to the secret garden up there on the cliff, once cultivated and loved by its sole founder. Only a select few knew of its existence, and I knew that we were blessed to have been shown the secret passage that led to this magical place. Marc and I had visited the Secret Garden not so long ago when we had desperately needed a moment alone in the chaos of the summer just gone.

I went alone this time, sitting on a bench made from a plank and two rocks, crying into the lily pond. I am a private mourner, and needed the solace of this special place where I could finally let go. I thank the one who made the garden for such a privileged space to be, at a time the whole world desperately wanted to help me but not one living man or woman could. No one witnessed those tears cried so hopelessly, so bitterly in that secret place as I sat huddled in my winter coat as the sky grew black.

A memorial was held for Marc where he used to work, at the Blue Bar in Porthtowan, overlooking the beach. To be honest, I can't remember much of it. All I can remember was that the place was full. Some local musicians wanted to put a CD together to raise money for the Balinese, called Blue Bali. I loved the idea, as did Carole and Ray. The Surf Club named the new rowing boat Blue Bali in Marc's honour. Two twin sisters Marc had known all his life sang a beautiful song for him. I said a few words on stage, something about how Marc always turned strangers into friends and lived each day to the full. I was doing my best, but still those words made me sick. I did not want to be saying these sort of tributes to Marc. I just wanted him to be alive.

The Blue Bar memorial did bring its own challenges. I finally met the girl I only knew as 'Nutty Nicky.' A girl-friend had pointed her out over the summer and told me that Marc was not the first 'taken' man the girl had tried to woo, from my friend's own experience. As I came out of the toilet Nutty Nicky was right there and we were forced to pass each other in the doorway. She was pretty and blonde with a small frame and freckles. We both paused as we passed, looking at each other uneasily. My heart thudded as I struggled to find some words to say. When the words spilled out, they were angry:

'I don't think you know how much trouble you've caused,' I said through gritted teeth, glaring at her. To my horror, she replied with what was almost a smirk.

'I think we've both been told different stories then,' she said, shrugging. How *could* she be so nonchalant? I wanted to kick her in the head and rip her hair out. Realising this was perhaps not the appropriate time and place for such activity, I carried on walking past with my head held high and lips pulled tight. But what the *hell* did she mean by that? What had Marc been saying? What was the truth and how could I ever truly know? He had sworn to me that nothing had ever happened, but this Nicky seemed to have a different view. And what about Naomi? Ah yes, she was there too.

As I came out of the toilet and glanced across the crowd-ed room I saw her sitting with her sister, who had also been a good friend of Marc's. I was doing my best to be kind to her. At the end of the day, she had been a close friend of his and I had to respect that. I did know that every night she lit a candle for Marc in her window, and I also knew from a mutual friend that she had been in love with him. There are no secrets in our village. She had brought her guitar along to the memorial and played some songs with Ray. Although I acknowledged it was a special moment for them, I don't think I quite had it in me to sing along this time.

With every week that passed, I truly believed they would be bringing Marc home but they never promised any time frame, other than, 'Shouldn't be too much longer'. So I waited in my state of limbo. The papers desperately wanted to know who the man was in the photo of me outside the Sari, which had by now been plastered in publications the world over. I just kept saying I didn't know (but of course I *wanted* to). After I had been in Cornwall for about two weeks I received a call from my parents who'd been contacted by the boy's parents. His name was Tom Singer and he was just seventeen years old. He'd suffered third degree burns to about seventy percent of his body.

I spoke with Tom's parents on the phone. They were so grateful that I had stopped to help him. Even though I could do nothing for Marc, in a way I felt relieved of some burden of grief. I had saved someone else's parents from that same pain I saw in Carole and Ray's eyes. His mother Megan told me he would have died there had I not pulled him away from the flames. Tom had spoken to Megan about me before he went into an induced coma. 'A lovely lady saved me,' he had said. Megan stayed in contact and sent me photos of Tom via e-mail. He was covered from head to toe in bandages, but he was *alive*.

I thought about Tom all the time and eagerly awaited updates on his progress. I learned that he was a bright, cheerful lad who was also a keen surfer. He had a sister and a brother he was very close to. I checked my email every day. Tom seemed to be progressing well, it was just going to take time. I looked forward to being able to visit him when I got back to Australia. Megan promised that I would be able to speak with him on the phone when he got better.

One day the phone rang at the Dobles, and Jenny passed the receiver on to me. At first I was happy to hear Megan's voice, until I heard a familiar broken tone. Tom had died of a stroke, not yet even eighteen years old.

As I placed the receiver down, despair once more washed over me like a kiss from the grim reaper, and my heart felt blacker and more hollow than before.

Chapter 11

Our Last Goodbye

I SAT DOWN WITH Ray and Carole several times a week, if they hadn't come to visit me for a cliff walk, or a meal with Gran. They were a source of strength for me, as I guess I was for them. Despite their own grief they treated me like a member of their family.

Marc's divorce papers finally come through only days after he had died, so he was still legally married at the time of his death. This added another whole complication to the legalities the family had to deal with. Still, the Gajardos were doing their best and managed to stay upbeat most of the time. They'd recently bought a camper and had decided to go on a big European trip when the winter subsided.

As I sat in their little lounge trying to eat my omelet, Carole cleaned up in the kitchen whilst Ray was speaking to me:

'When Marc sang in harmony with my vocals or played guitar to my voice, we blended together so beautifully,' he said sadly, shaking his head in disbelief. Since Marc had died, Ray had stopped playing the guitar. He looked up at me with tired eyes: 'I miss him every waking moment, Hanabeth. Just when I think things are getting better, something throws me off balance. I came across his tools in the garage again yesterday and when I saw his surfboard in the outhouse today I broke down again.' Ray shook his head, 'What are we going to *do*, Kid?'

I had to do *something*. It was now mid-November, and I was going spare with grief and confusion. All I wanted was to somehow say goodbye to Marc. *'See you in a bit'*, was hardly a goodbye of any sort. I prayed daily that he could somehow come and find me. I'd never seen a ghost, but in the past I had experienced dreams that I felt had somehow connected with another dimension. I prayed and begged Marc to do whatever he could just to come and say goodbye to me.

The sun struggled to break though the clouds. I had a mission in hand as I wound my way through the gorse down from the Dobles to Trevaunance Point. It had been raining so my rubber-soled ugg boots slipped on the mud. I walked down stairs that cut into the cliff until I was right out on the point. The wind was howling offshore, so I climbed down a short way to a ledge that was protected from the wind. I had brought with me a candle, a CD player and a red rose.

I huddled on my perch looking out over the dark blue sea and the grey wispy sky. I pressed play on my little blue Walkman and watched the disk start to spin. Jeff Buckley sung from the speakers, which I could only just hear above the waves breaking on the rocks below. I kneeled to light a candle and incense in tribute to Balinese tradition. I unraveled a long narrow strip of paper, and to the wind and the gulls I read a letter I'd written for Marc.

When I'd finished, I carefully rolled the letter around the thorny stem of the rose and Jeff Buckley's 'Last Goodbye' started to play. I inhaled the rich scent of the rose and closed my eyes. I had taken care to find a rose with a strong scent and large thorns.

'I love you,' I whispered as I let the velvet petals of the rose touch my face, as if to imagine the brush of a kiss. 'Like this rose, it seems that the fullest of life must be experienced for its best and worst, for its beautiful colour, its rich scent and its bloody sharp thorns. I'm sorry you had to go so soon, but thank you for all of the love, the beauty of the times we shared, the lessons we learnt and the challenges we overcame together. I understand that you have to go, I know that somehow this has to be, but my god I miss you by my side... I *miss* you.' Huge tears rolled down my cheeks as I spoke, but I maintained my composure as I stood on the cliff ledge, clutching the rose.

'Please be free, do what you have to do on your next adventure, but there is one thing: Please, if you have any way to come and see me in a dream, please come to say goodbye, just one last time. I need this... Please, please Marc.' I held out the rose and let it fall with my tears to join the seething waters below. As I watched it fall into the water, Lilac Wine started to play and I sat there alone, lost deep in my own silence.

It was not long until my prayer was answered. He chose to come and see me at the Eden Project, an environmental park made up of huge geodesic structured bio-domes. The biggest one overflowed with lush tropical greenery, while it's smaller neighbor had a Mediterranean climate filled with cork trees and citrus bushes. I'd always wanted to go and see it but had never yet been in my waking life. I was there with a big group of friends including Laurs and Matt, Nicola and Lian. We were walking up a wide staircase with a red carpet between the two bio-domes and Marc stood to the right at the top of the stairs waiting patiently for me.

'Hanabeth,' he called to me quietly. I glanced over to him and then back at the group, concerned about losing them in the bustling crowd. He stepped forwards and said my name again, louder this time.

'Hanabeth. Don't worry about them. They're all okay.' He gestured back down below to where Laurs and Nic were walking, only they were now smiling old ladies, walking side by side. He spoke urgently to get my attention: 'It's *me*, Marc!' Startled, and suddenly realising what was happening, I looked back at Marc and stepped towards him, bewildered as he took my hand.

'Marc, you came! It's really you!' As I hugged him I looked into his dark eyes and I could smell his hair, feel his beautiful velvet skin at my fingertips as his warm embrace encircled my cold body. Every sense was vivid and so, so real.

Marc took my hand and led me to the tropical dome where we were hidden from the crowd under some banana palms by a wooden hut. There we sat down close together for the last time, talking through the pain and the love we had shared. Finally, Marc stood up, pulling me up gently with him, and now his face had the saddest look I had ever seen.

'Is this really goodbye?' I asked as he pulled me close, looking up to him, feeling his lips in my hair.

'Don't, please. Just don't,' he whispered, kissing me gently. I ran my fingers through his hair and pulled my arms around him, inhaling his scent. We clung together in a strong embrace, and hugged tighter than we ever had, as if we were never to let go. I buried my face against the fabric of his t-shirt, feeling every sense as if through a magnifying glass. We stayed in a tight embrace for a long time until I started to cry. I awoke in my bed at the Dobles and for a long while I could still feel the pressure and the warmth of his arms around me as I sobbed in the morning sun that flooded in through the skylights.

By the end of November, I was starting to lose the plot. Again, I rang the Australian consulate and asked when Marc was going to be sent home.

'It should be within a couple of weeks,' came the response.

'You said that *six* weeks ago! *How* much longer? We identified him *there*. I can't bear to wait any more!'

'I'm sorry, only the next of kin could have officially identified him.' They had already unsuccessfully tried dental identification and had now taken DNA swabs from Ray.

'Bloody red tape. Unbelievable!' I cried as I hung up the receiver. Lian walked over and comforted me, rubbing my back.

'I guess they have to be sure,' she said, ever pragmatic. I had gone to visit her and her dairy farmer boyfriend up near Bristol.

'Lian, I'm sooo frustrated. I'm so bored! I wish I could do something constructive, something good with my time here. I'd like to raise some money for Bali to help them out somehow.'

'Hmm...' I looked up at Lian who had her thinking face on. 'Why don't you organise a charity surf contest?' she said, smiling. I jumped up from my chair and hugged her.

'Whoo! You're a genius! That's exactly what I'll do. I'll make a plan, and I'll ring Minnow.' Lian smiled happily and handed me a pen and notebook. I drew a sketch of what I wanted to plan, including a music night and a raffle. I rang Minnow, a friend and Aggie character who happened to be the local expert in organising surf contests.

'No worries, Hanabeth!' was the first thing he said in his broad Cornish accent, before rattling off a list of what I had to do next. I rang the British Surfing Association (BSA) and they were keen to help too, as were my friends at Carve Magazine. After a few more phone calls that met with similar responses, I had it all planned, and the date was set for the winter solstice. It seemed that everybody wanted to help in any way they could, so it came together quickly. The next day I finally received the phone call I had been waiting for: Marc's body was coming home.

On the November morning of Marc's Funeral, the sky was a crisp cold blue. It was exactly two months after the bomb had gone off far away in the chaos of Kuta. The frosty grass crunched under our feet and the trees were bare of leaves. I saw a little robin redbreast sitting on the wall across from the chapel of rest, watching us as we funneled into the white building. James Taylor's 'Close your Eyes' was playing as we made our way to our seats.

The crematorium was completely overflowing with people both young and old. There were a lot of young folk from Aggie and Porthtowan. I sat down next to Carole and Ray and looked up to see the wooden box a couple of metres in front of me, holding what was left of the beautiful warm body I had once held so close. Several members of Marc's family spoke a few words, and Marc's cousin spoke of how all of the clocks in his house had stopped on the night of the bomb, even his wrist-watch. It's funny, I thought, how these sorts of coincidences no longer surprised me. The same thing had happened at Tommy's. The clocks had all stopped at 11:14 pm that night.

Carole and so many others could not stop crying, but my eyes were still dry for much of the ceremony. Then came Whitney: a song I'd usually consider cheesy, but as she started to belt out '*I will always love you*', there was no stopping the tears. There must have been more than three hundred people wailing and sobbing during that long-awaited moment. I saw Dave the Rave close by. His black suit contrasted with the last time I'd seen him in his floral shirt and flares with a huge smile on a Newquay dance floor.

Of course Lian and Andy had come down, as had my sister Melanie who'd flown over from Italy, although she felt sad to have never actually had the chance to meet Marc. Gran sat to my left and Lian and Melanie sat behind me. Seeing the grief on Gran's face was so hard, because I knew that she too had loved him dearly. I meant the world to her, and she'd been so happy when she'd met Marc and seen us together. I glanced across at her, sitting neatly as ever with her perfectly permed curls and matching smart grey suit. She clutched her hankie in her hand as she stared ahead and wept quietly.

'It's just so awful…' she whispered between her tears.

It was only a few more days until we held 'Surf for Bali' down at Aggie beach. I'm pretty sure it was the first surf contest that had been held on the winter solstice. Fortunately the sky was clear blue and although the waves were small they were as clean as a whistle. My old workplace Schooners provided a perfect hangout for the contest. All the judges lined up on wooden stools beside the big paned windows along the front of the building. The polished wooden floors quickly became sandy as surfers, judges, organisers and general tea drinkers filled the place. The whole BSA was there with all of the best surfers in Britain.

Everybody had wanted to provide support in any way they could as the local surfing community had strong ties with Bali. It was fortunate really that our community had not lost more people in the blast. Afterwards, it was time to let off steam (well, warm up) upstairs at the Driftwood, to celebrate the success of the day by sinking some nice warm ale. Skinners had put on the beers and so everyone who had entered the contest was making the most of it in true Cornish fashion.

This was the first time I'd been out in a crowded place like this, so it was bound to be a bit of a challenge. As the band started I eyed the exits nervously, glugging on my pint, as people kept pouring into the large low-ceilinged room. After a couple of songs we started the prize-giving and the raffle. I handed out the prizes, and the most prestigious was the Marc Gajardo memorial trophy, which had been made and donated for the purpose. As Marc had always loved girls being out in the water and had been so supportive of my surfing, it was decided that it would be given to the winner of the ladies.

By the end of the day we had raised about $12,000. We sent it off to Bali via the Rotary Club to go towards updating the hospital facilities at Sanglah. Not bad for a couple of weeks worth of phone calls (*and a whole unified community*).

For the first time since the Sari Club I took to the smoky dance floor, placing one foot in front of the other and then moving the other foot again. I smiled and tried to look as if it was easy and natural, yet the truth was that dancing seemed like the hardest thing to do in the world. My feet were like lead, and I felt sick in my stomach. With every step I held Marc in my heart and promised him and myself that I would bloody keep dancing, for him and for all those who could never dance again.

Christmas was spent amongst the refuge of the warm chatter and smiles of the extensive Doble family. All the boys were home, as was Lian and many of the cousins, uncles and aunties. We all ploughed down Rocky Lane together to jump in the sea for the traditional 11am swim in our bathers. I cheated by putting on some wetsuit boots with my bikini and paddled out with Marc's board to catch some perfect three-foot waves. I wasn't wearing a leash so I can tell you that I was feeling the cold after swimming in to retrieve the board for the third time (in water below twelve degrees). It was worth it though, and after twenty minutes or so I came in as Carole and Ray met me on the shore. I walked with them and the rest of the Dobles up the steep hill to the Driftwood to collect the free mulled wine, reserved for all of those who braved the icy waters of the Christmas swim. We gathered around the great table of polished wood, and I sat there staring at the scene around me, pondering the life that had passed since Marc and I had sat together under the great fig tree outside the Nutshed in 40 degree heat, exactly twelve months before.

My flight was booked to return to Australia on New Years Eve. A couple of days before I left I received a call from Ray:

'The conditions are perfect, Kid. Shall we pick you up or shall we meet you down there?'

'Pick me up, please,' I replied.

We wound our way around the large stones and rocks, down onto the sand. We'd timed it well and the tide was perfect, out far past the points. Days of rain and wind had swept the land and sky pure and clean. The sand was free of footprints as we rounded the corner, feeling the offshore wind drop as we met the shelter of the tall black cliffs. We were all wearing wetsuits with our coats over the top. Ray carried a tall red plastic box, Carole carried a ring of orange and yellow flowers, and together Steve and I carried a surfboard shaped wreath that had been made of blue flowers to look like Marc's board. We circled the large pools of deep green water that surrounded the rocks, reaching the pink-coloured cliffs and the cathedral cave to see the engine house of Wheal Coates standing high above us on the cliff-top.

My mind flashed back to a sunny day years before when Marc had sat in the open window looking out over this same shimmering blue sea. As we stood on the water's edge I put my hand in my pocket to feel the photo I still carried from that day. I pulled it out and held it up to my face, looking at the contemplative, peaceful expression on Marc's handsome young face, a face that will never grow old.

We started to wade out through the white water. Although it was a small swell the waves were consistent and it took some effort for Ray and Carole, who were not accustomed to the ocean, to wade out to where the waves were breaking. Just as I was wondering how we would get out without destroying the wreaths, the swell stopped and the waves parted, revealing crystal-green water. We pushed the wreaths out towards the horizon, to be caught by the offshore breeze. Ray opened the red box and offered it to each of us in turn. Without a word, Carole reached in and took a handful.

'We love you forever, Marc,' she said, as she let the ashes blow through her fingers into the ocean, crying the tears that only a mother who has outlived her child can cry.

Carole giggled as she peeled herself out of the borrowed wetsuit. Ray, too, laughed. It was good to see them smile. I think we were all feeling relieved after the long period we'd been living in limbo. Huddled together in their campervan, Steve's girlfriend made us a cup of steaming hot tea to warm our frozen fingers. Sipping on the warm liquid, it finally felt like my time here in these windy hills was over: I had done everything I had come back to do and it was time to fly back to warmer waters. On our way back around the Beacon to the Dobles we pulled into Wheal Coates to look down on the expanse of shimmering ocean. Ray and I were chatting as Carole walked ahead with Steve.

'Oooh, look!' cried Carole as she pointed, and sure enough we could see the brightly-coloured wreaths in the water far below us slowly drifting their way to the western horizon on an open sea.

Chapter 12

Keep on Dancing

What is the dancefloor when you're dancing with
a broken heart?
What are the lights, who cares about the songs? Not I.
Hollow the tunes play and your feet move, you sway.
Try to keep the smile on your face.
But it's not on, feels so wrong. You're gone.
It's a farce to dance as your heart is breaking.
But you have to sway to the beat.
There's no other way to make it through.
But the song stops and you break free,
Because the beat is gone, it just can't be.
The heart does beat on, and its not always wrong,
To dance with a broken heart, but sometimes,
Just every now and then, the music stops.

I FLEW STRAIGHT INTO the Gold Coast on New
Year's Eve. Weekends blurred in to one long hazy
party. Gary Charles from the Byron Liquor Commit-

tee called around one day to let us know that they'd put a hat around the pubs in Byron Bay just after the bomb. As a result they'd collected a few thousand dollars for our family and for the family of Jodi Wallace, who had also been killed in the Bali bomb. I thought about it, and suggested that perhaps the money could go towards an eye operation for my short sight, which had been a long-term dream of mine. I continually lost/scratched/sat on my glasses and struggled with my contact lenses, especially in the surf where I dreamed of opening my eyes underwater without losing my contacts. In this way, the people who had donated could see it going to something tangible, and Gary agreed.

I went in to Barry Wallace's shop. I guess I just wanted to say hello. Barry was Jodi's father, and it broke my heart to see the eyes of another grieving father. It reminded me again that all over Australia, and in thirty-three countries all over the world, were fathers with eyes like Barry Wallace's, like Ray Gajardo's, like Peter Singer's. Mother's eyes like Carole's, brothers like Steve's. No fanfare, just emptiness.

Others lived with the memories of that night, and on the Gold Coast I met up with a couple of the guys who'd survived. I'd been uninjured but they had not been so lucky. I met up with Glenn, the man who Bobby had described with a snapped leg. His leg was still in a huge metal frame with spokes pushing into his flesh. His friend Andy was in a wheelchair with one leg and his other foot missing. The physical wounds were still fresh, yet most of us had not even begun to contemplate how it would affect us inside, what the flames, the pain and the loss would do to us. Through the grape vine I heard news of many survivors and how they were (or weren't) coping. Some used their grief as a catalyst for good, for change, for helping others. Others were still unable to help themselves. Some froze up. Some gave up.

Despite my determination to forge forwards, I was still spinning without a compass. I stayed between Tommy's place at Miami on the Gold Coast and Mum and Dad's place in Byron. There was talk of going to war with Iraq, and so I spoke at a Peace march in Byron to several thousand people. I didn't want *any* more violence. Tommy had a great idea for me to organise a big festival called 'Peace Aid', and I did start making a few phone calls to festival organisers and musicians. I started to liaise with Sting's girlfriend Trudie Styler (this thing really could have kicked off). Although I probably could have pulled it together, I was starting to realise that I really wanted to somehow get myself back a bit closer to the ground, to reality, whatever that was.

I remember very little of this time: I have hazy memories of a dance floor, just dancing my time away, slipping up to the smoky bar for an occasional tequila, then back through the thick crowd of people busy in their own summer fun, smoking joints and sinking deeper and deeper into my own haze. I danced as if it was all I had left, with Tommy and his friends standing close by. My haze was disrupted intermittently by bouts of deep sadness, frustration and anger, and my family bore the full brunt of it. When I sobered up, I felt vulnerable and skinless.

In short, I was unreasonable and unstable, on an emotional rollercoaster with no idea which way it was going to twist next.

'Why can't there just be food in the house!' I screamed at my mother. 'Nothing! Why can't you at least provide me with food? It's hard enough just trying to keep myself going. I'm wasting away! Not even any fruit. I hate this house!'

Hearing the bratty tone of my voice and having a pretty good idea of how unreasonable I was being, I struggled to shut up, but the words just kept spewing from my mouth:

'Basic nourishment! You can't expect me to eat this healthy shit that tastes as interesting as a cardboard box! I can't believe you have to buy this milk! I hate it! I told you so many times which one I like!' I was shouting now, shouting over my mother's lack of fondness for shopping. In retrospect she was trying hard. She didn't even drink milk.

'This is no way to speak to me, Hanabeth. It's just not on!' she replied angrily. I picked up the milk and tipped it into the sink. I threw the carton in the bin, glaring at Mother. Hearing a knock sounding at the door, I heard Andy call up the stairs.

'Helooo, is it safe to come up?!' I shut up. Pretty good timing, actually. God knows what I would have found to yell about next.

Andy took one look at me and started singing my name and grinning. 'Hanabeth, Hanabeth, Hanabeth!'

I growled in response. 'I hate this place. I've half a mind to just drive to Western Australia tomorrow ... if my car was bloody working,' I was still carless and it was just another reason why I was well on my way to going stir crazy, heavily dependent on my family. Andy looked at me again and said:

'Come on. Let's go see the sea!'

'Please! Take her away!' Mum interjected as she received another hot glare from me.

We sat in his van as he sped down the road. I felt anger and stress leaching out of my eyeballs, my whole body tense, my back aching. After a few minutes Andy spoke:

'You're being pretty nasty to your mum, dude.'

'Bugger off. She's a pain in the arse and I can't stand living there. Her and Dad just don't stop bickering over the most insignificant crap. I can't believe I'm living with my parents again. I'm hungry. I want a Mexican pie,' I demanded as we pulled up to Macs' burger bar. 'She can't even keep food in the house when I hardly eat as it is,' I complained.

'Have you ever considered doing some shopping?' asked Andy calmly. I stared at him blankly, not quite understanding the concept. 'You're a pain in the arse when you haven't been fed,' he said finally.

We jumped back into the car loaded with pies and chocolate milk. Driving through Byron, I sighed in exasperation at the people all over the town, meandering all over the road in front of us, lost in their holiday bliss.

'I hate summer in Byron.' I whinged. Andy ignored me.

We checked the surf at a couple of beaches and decided to paddle out at Wategos, each on Marc's longboards. Andy lugged 'the Log', a 9'6" triple redwood stringer while I balanced Marc's favourite, a pale green 9'3" volan glass Noosa '66 on my head.

The surf was clean and small. We waded up to our waists before plunging in to the cool water, pleasantly refreshing on our skin after the hot summer sun. I jumped onto the board and paddled quickly out past the waves. Once again, the water cooled my troubled mind as I rode wave after wave, tracing Marc's steps up and down the board, feeling it turning slowly with the shifting of my weight. My heart eased as we sat smiling and chatting with the other surfers, all different sorts of people just out in the crystal waters to share the best life can offer. Watching the dolphins playing just metres away, I figured my life was really not that bad.

In the ocean I felt somehow closer to Marc, gliding on his board. I could feel him there with me, guiding me along. Although I had never been a longboard rider before, on his board I felt confident and calm. The board moved the way I wanted it to and I almost felt his style and grace in my own movements. The best waves seemed to come easily to me. It was weird, in the nicest way.

Still, the real world had a way of creeping back in.

I saw Australian PM John Howard on the TV using the terror attack in Bali as a justification for the war in Iraq, and I was infuriated. A newspaper headline, "88 reasons to go to war in Iraq," inspired me write a letter to the Australian (at least eighty-eight Australians had been killed in the bombing). To this, I knew I must clearly say, *'Not in my name'*. I believed we were in danger of further alienating the Islamic community, making them feel persecuted, and therefore more angry and desperate.

This wasn't going to lead to a solution, and besides, there was *no link* with Bali! Through losing Marc and experiencing the bomb, I had realised the true brutality of such violence and the resulting domino effect on people's lives. I wanted to better understand the causes of this anger and resentment against us. If we were looking for positive change and an end to this sort of hatred, I believed that we needed to start treating other cultures with respect before they were going to respect us.

If governments can afford to blow the world up, why can't they see instead that each person has their essential needs met and that our environment is cared for? If we are going to involve ourselves in the affairs of other countries, why not provide aid and assistance, not bombs and more hatred? Little did I realise, I was about to get a chance to put my case forward.

I was on the way to my car with a hand-full of bikinis when I received a call from a producer in London.

'Hi Hanabeth. What are you doing tomorrow?' she asked.

'Driving to Western Australia, why?'

'Would you be able to come to England instead, to speak with Tony Blair?'

'Ummm … sure. Do you think it's possible to fly me back via WA?'

'That can be arranged. See you soon.'

'Okay.'

Chapter 13

Blair's Bad Day at the Office

A S WE MARCHED over Westminster Bridge the winter sky swirled grey over the ancient city, whipping cold air straight through my inadequate clothing. Looking down at the dark turbulent waters of the Thames, I realised just how far I was from the crystal blue-green ocean of Byron Bay. It was only days since I'd been surfing along the sub-tropical shoreline, wearing colourful summer clothes and laughing with my friends. Now everything was cold and grey, and there was a serious task at hand. On all sides of me strode seventeen equally determined women, all of whom had been selected for various reasons to be on the TV show 'Tonight with Trevor McDonald", as part of a group who were about to face the British Prime Minister, Tony Blair.

The women came from a wide variety of backgrounds. Some had husbands and children in the British Army, which was waiting for the starting whistle to sound in Iraq. Some were in the army themselves, and one lady's husband was a human shield in Iraq at that moment. Two grey-haired women had lost their sons in the twin towers in New York. There was an activist from Edinburg and several Muslim women, including one Iraqi who had lived in London for many years. We discovered that together we were united by one thing, and that was our deep concern about the pending war in Iraq, poised to start in a week (*without* the support of the UN).

The cockney accent of the producer called out loudly above the noise of the traffic:

'CUT! CUT! No, no you're all looking far too cheerful. You can talk but *don't* tell jokes! Try to walk more as a group this time.' There was a collective sigh as we ambled back, preparing to walk over the bridge for the tenth time that day. I observed the city around me as Big Ben loomed above, and the Houses of Parliament stretched out along the northern riverbank. Everywhere I looked there were old, tired grey buildings on grey streets under a grey sky. The river seemed to be the only relic of a natural environment left (I am *not* a city girl).

We moved faster, anxious to get the day's shooting over and done with. It seemed odd that they had to spend a whole day shooting us walking about, while we would only have one hour with the Prime minister tomorrow, but that's TV for you. They *had* flown me from Australia, after all.

'That's it, one more time. We need to film you from another angle,' the producer piped up again. I shivered as we stopped on the top of the bridge and a sharp gust swirled the litter on the pavement into a tiny whirlwind. An Iraqi woman with a beautiful smile offered me her jacket for the third time, and this time I gratefully took it, laughing at my lack of preparedness for this weather.

They filmed us walking past the Queen's mounted guards and crossing Downing Street. They stopped the flood of pedestrians on the wide pavements of Whitehall so we could march ten metres down the street with the camera crew following us from the centre of the road. We jumped onto a heated coach for coffee and biscuits between filming, chatting away with the production team and the other women.

At 10 am the next day we boarded a coach to the foreign office. We walked through the archway into the grey court-yard, with the sound of high heels on cobbles resonating off the walls. As we climbed the thick red carpets of the State Stair, I tried to take in all of the intricate murals painstakingly detailed in rich colours, angels adorned with gold paint. We walked over a mosaic floor under a succession of golden archways until we came to the high door that was opened for us.

As we waited for the Prime Minister, the atmosphere in the room grew tense, the seconds ticking by on the gold clock on the fire place behind Trevor Macdonald, the presenter. He sat in front waiting patiently. He was used to this. I sat in the middle of the semi-circle of women, waiting not so patiently. After 3,627 seconds, Blair finally arrived.

First I heard the voice I had heard so many times before on the news, on the TV and on the radio. He sounded louder and more posh than I expected. Perhaps that was because he was about a foot away.

'Sorry to be late,' Blair said apologetically as he dusted lint off his dark grey suit. He had a strong presence without uttering another word. I could almost feel the intense energy that can only belong to a man who is deciding the fate of millions.

I could feel tensions rising as the women around me gathered their thoughts. The lips of some trembled under the hot lights. Blair turned, looking up at us as he sat down. I almost felt sorry for him, staring up into the eyes of eighteen intelligent and emotional women sat in a semi-circle. We had already spent two days and nights bonding during the preparation for the show. He knew this was not going to be easy.

Trevor introduced the program and we were off. One by one he introduced each woman, inviting her to pose a question to the Prime Minister. Under the eye of the cameras and the heat of the lights, the onslaught began. The temperature rose and Tony Blair began to perspire.

Trevor Macdonald had much to say and our time was cut significantly by their friendly banter, serving only to frustrate the women further. One woman sat patiently with her hand raised. She currently had all her sons serving in the British Military in Iraq. She'd told us yesterday that she felt let down, that their lives were at risk for the wrong reasons. Her hand grew tired but Trevor did not pick her to speak, and some of the more vocal women in the room had much to say. Eventually I couldn't help it. I burst out, almost rudely:

'Please, let her speak!' I felt I had to help the quietly spoken lady have her moment.

We took a break. Blair took a sip of his water and glanced around. A production assistant came up and wiped the beads of sweat from his brow and dabbed some make up on his face.

I regarded him coolly. What possessed him to agree to this? Did he think if he could convince these women that he was doing the right thing in Iraq, perhaps he could convince the country, maybe even himself?

'I believe what I am doing is right,' was his well-worn sentence as we began again.

I stared hard into his eyes, not a stare of anger but one of curiosity. I was looking for the signs of a liar. I was looking for a hint of himself beyond the worn-out sentences. I don't know how many times I heard the term 'weapons of mass destruction'. His eyes flicked from woman to woman, but what struck me was a deep weariness and sadness I saw behind the mask. When he repeated again that he believed in his actions, finally I realised that I just didn't believe him. Regardless, a man must answer for his actions, and I was in just the mood to ask the right questions.

As the hour drew quickly on, the emotions in the room were fit to bursting. The women had gathered their thoughts and were realising that the time was running out for them to share their urgent message. I knew mine was saved for last, so my brain was whirring.

Finally, I posed my question:

'I've come from Australia to show you this photograph that was taken of Marc Gajardo and myself. It was taken on the eleventh of October last year, the night before the Bali Bomb. We were both in the Sari Club, Marc was killed and I made it out. I've seen the carnage and the devastation and the suffering that results for families in Australia and in England. I heard the thud of Marc's father's knees as he fell to the floor when I told him that his son was dead. All this is the consequence of *just one bomb*. Do you *really* want to support Bush and go into this war with Iraq and subject so many more innocent Iraqi families to the same pain that I have seen? *Regardless* of how accurate your bombs are, they *will* be killed, and they *will* be hurt. Do you *really* believe this is justified? They are going to become more desperate and *then* may resort to more terrorism. Do you not believe this is going to be a consequence of the war on Iraq where more innocents will be killed?'

'If they were able to get hold of even worse material than they used in Bali, you could talk about not several hundred but several thousand dying,' Blair argued. 'I genuinely believe that there is a real risk, and that the sort of terrorist groups that perpetrated the atrocity in Bali are trying to get hold of these weapons and that people will die on a massive scale.'

Undeterred, I pressed on with my argument. 'Until we start asking *why* they hate us so much, we are not going to find out why this is occurring. These people are not *using* "weapons of mass destruction." They are using weapons that are at their hands easily. They used *planes* to destroy the World Trade Centre; they used *fertilizer* in Bali. They are using their minds, not "weapons of mass destruction".'

Blair paused slightly as his gaze met mine. When he spoke, he stammered: 'Well, surely you must agree with me on one thing, that if they could use weapons of mass destruction, they would?'

One woman's hand had been raised for the full hour, and she never did get her chance to speak. She left devastated that she had been through all of that in vain. She did, however, join us in a slow handclap as the meeting drew to a close.

After the show was over and the cameras stopped rolling, I walked up to Blair clutching the photograph. I stopped about a metre away and held out the image of the tanned faces and white smiling teeth of Marc and I holding up our drinks at dinner at the Puri Dajuma. On the back was written: 'Marc and Hanabeth: 11th October 2002.' I spoke quietly this time, with urgency in my voice.

'I know that you have children, Mr Blair. I would like you to look at this photo and imagine for just a moment that this was your son Euan or your daughter Kathryn sitting there at that table. How would you feel if you lost them? How would you *feel* if it was your son Nicky poised right now to fight in Iraq?' I fought back the tears and my eyes shone as I stared straight into Blair's blue eyes, feeling the force of millions standing behind my quiet words. 'I assure you, Mr Blair, that had you seen the pain, death and destruction that I have seen from just one bomb, you would be doing everything in your power to ensure that not *one* more bomb was let loose on human life. An eye for an eye and the whole world goes blind. If not with *you*, where and when is this ever going to stop?'

Blair took the photo and slowly walked away to make a decision that would affect many generations to come.

Back in the sanctum of the Driftwood, I'd just sat down wearily for a Cornish ale surrounded by friends, chuckling at the front page of *'The Scotsman'* where Blair and I stood face to face: 'Blair's Bad Day at the Office', said the headline. Apparently it had also appeared on the front of *the Australian*, with the headline 'Blair Sweats for Peace'. As I put down the paper to take my first delicious sip, Jill leaned over the bar:

'Anabeth, you've got a phone call my love.' Confused, I excused myself and picked up the receiver. It was a producer from an Australian current affairs program.

'Hi Hanabeth, what are you doing tomorrow?'

'I was planning on not much.'

'Can you get to London first thing?'

'Not really, it's a fair way away. Why?'

'Can you do the same thing you did with Blair with John Howard?' I sighed, then took a deep breath before I answered:

'Sounds like a great opportunity. I'd love to.'

This time was very different and things didn't quite go according to plan. Firstly, I'd been flown up to London with a friend and we'd raided the mini-bar in the Radisson the night before. It was a very early start to make the live satellite linkup with Australia and I tried not to look too bleary-eyed as the makeup artist let loose on my face and hair. The second error was that I gave no resistance. In fact, as I glanced in the mirror I thought I looked pretty good, although admittedly nothing like myself. Perhaps more like a teen-pop star than anything, with pink lipstick and plenty of blusher.

I sat waiting for the link-up with a picture of the London skyline on the wall behind me, thinking about the questions I would shortly be posing to the Australian Prime Minister. What no one had mentioned to me that morning was that Howard had decided to back out of the interview at the last minute. I found out later that he had faced one of the lowest ebbs in his popularity that day when he had been egged in Adelaide, and so had decided to stand me up.

When the live link-up began, I was thrown completely off guard when the reporter asked the question:

'If you had the chance to speak with Howard, what would you say?' It was a small technical difference to what I had been expecting, but any eloquence I had dribbled straight out of me. Rather than asking, 'Why, am I not go-ing to be speaking with him directly as planned?' I tried to keep the show going. It wasn't awful, but I cringed later when I saw the footage of me done up like a princess trying to make a few poorly worded points.

By lunchtime I was walking down a busy Oxford Street with a friend, wandering in and out of the shops, buying stuff I didn't need. We had just spent an hour in the biggest clothes shop I'd ever seen: a girls' paradise with acres of funky clothes, shoes, belts and handbags. Coming up to an odd little shop, a man stood on the doorstep with some sort of gadget that looked like a white funnel attached to a drum. As we passed by he set it off, and there was a sudden rush of warm air. Without hesitating, I dove to the ground and pulled my friend with me, covering my head. I crouched for a second, giving us both a close view of the cobbled pavement. The man stared at us. Once I realised there had been no explosion, I immediately burst into tears, both from relief, and from anger that I had made myself look so stupid. My friend looked at me in confusion as she dusted herself off, as did the rest of the people hurrying past.

It turned out that our trip to London had been in vain in more ways than one. Sixty million people around the world had marched in the name of peace, but not the eighteen women, nor the UN, nor *sixty million people* could affect the deadly decision that had already been made by a handful of men. The day I left England Tony Blair, George Bush and John Howard had already started to drop bombs on Iraq.

Chapter 14

The Wave at the End of the Earth

To bare one's soul to the world,
To throw one's care to the wind,
To be what you have become,
Read the verse written on your heart.
Succumb to your wildest dreams,
Reach for the freedom you feel inside
And play, play through the day,
Let the tide pull your worries away.
Ride the wave of life,
Through barrels, over flat spots.
Carve the turns that become your past
And leave a trail of rainbow spray.
For the wave will break and pass,
Make the memory worth being something that lasts.
You can choose your waves each day,
Make sure you ride them smooth, long and fast.

THE SUN SHONE bright, reflected from the sparkling turquoise ocean around the sand, rocks and shrubs of the bay. As she sank slowly towards the ocean, the glow of orange and pink was bounced straight back out to sea by the big sheet windows of the cluster of houses on the hill. A group of young and invariably barefoot surfers sat on the wooden steps leading down to the beach, sipping on beer, discussing the waves and events of the day. It was all new and perfect. At that moment, anything was possible and my only expression was a smile, whether excited and stoked from a great wave, or dreamy and tired, considering the endless possibilities of my life. It was as if my memory had been temporarily wiped clean. I was anonymous, just another girl travelling in a van. As infinite as the fluid ocean stretching out before me was my new chance of living.

Most of the crowd around me I'd met that day. A slim and beautiful French woman with long dark hair sat laughing on the step of her camper van, cigarette in hand, chatting away with the Aussie swagman, a rare but ancient type of drifter, smiling and animated as he swigged his Emu Bitter out of a brown paper bag.

The conversation of the group wandered from our differing origins, through our travels and of course to foreign waves. We would probably all stay parked right there, crawling into our vans after a few more beers, guitar songs and pasta cooked over a camp stove. I gazed back to the white Mazda van I'd hired in Perth, wishing I owned it. Lost in my own world as usual, I was drifting in my mind out to the purple-pink waves peeling in perfectly curved lines around the point.

A cheerful local bloke came up the steps with his surfboard, and invited us all to a party that night. Sorted. Life was moving and flowing, things falling into place in their own time as the minutes slipped away into hours, days and months.

I'd headed to Western Australia looking for wide open spaces and new shores, and found them in abundance. I stayed a short while in Perth, picked up from the airport in an immaculate orange Kombie by Ant, an old friend from Cornwall. He gave me an easy introduction to Western Australia and took me sailing on his catamaran at Fremantle. I stayed with his family for a few days and cooked them Cornish pasties to say thanks. I threw my surfboard and backpack into the hired white van to drive southwards on a very straight, very long stretch of highway. I passed wide expanses of scrub and dry fields scattered with occasional farms and small towns as the hot dry air rushed past the open window. I was singing.

'It's time to move on, it's time to get going... what lies ahead I have no way of knowing...' Four hours later I pulled up at Surfers Point, or what they call Main Break, Margaret River. The sun was easing down, hovering just above the horizon in a pale pink cloudless sky. Seagulls swooped overhead and settled on a low wooden fence. I stood watching the waves. It was a bit too late to paddle out, but all the same my heart was soaring. How long had I dreamed of coming to this place? A long, long time, and now I was finally sitting right here, and the endless possibilities of the waves that lined the coast took my breath away.

Here, there were no photos to remind me. No TVs were blaring out unwelcome news. No one was asking questions. To the people here, I was just a young blow-in with an English accent here for the waves. All the belongings I had would fit straight back into my backpack if and when I wanted them to.

The newspapers no longer knew where I was. No television crews would ever stand on this doorstep. Finally I was free of labels like 'Bombgirl'; 'Bali Survivor' and; 'Lost her boyfriend…' I heaved a sigh of relief. No one was going to come up to me with those sad eyes and say, 'I'm so sorry…'

It was now six months since the bomb had changed everything. I needed to once more feel down my body and check that my feet were in tact, and find out where they were standing. I needed to see, after all the media attention and chaos that my life had become, what had been left in my place? *Who* was this girl who had experienced something so powerful that it changes 'We' to 'I' in an instant. I was battling a life without Marc's presence, yet I could not picture his face in my mind. I had a vague idea, but I did not realise how numb I had become. I was amazed how quickly I'd appeared to bounce back, and at the fact that I seemed 'fine'. The wind blew off my troubles, and the rest of my cares were dissolved beneath the waves. Emotionally though, I barely existed.

There is something very powerful about being alone in a vast space. For me it is intensely healing and comforting. I stood on the empty shore, out of breath from a sprint up the sand. I climbed up onto on a rock poking up where the dunes met the cliff. There was no sound but the heavy crashing waves on the rocks below as the wind tore joyfully at my hair. The barren but beautiful coast stretched out before me with not one house nor human as far as I could see, and that was a long way. I felt exhilarated: I felt so alone, and wild and free.

I heard from the 'Old Boys' standing by their cars, that a big swell was coming so I got directions to a supposedly mellow wave called 'South Point', before heading into the Margaret River pub to earn myself a hangover. I woke up to birds chirping at the crack of dawn, finding myself horribly dehydrated. I rummaged around in the back of the van for a bottle of water. After glugging down a litre or so, I hauled myself into the driver's seat. The directions seemed pretty straight-forward as I drove down the tree-lined roads. Everywhere, kangaroos bounced across the fields and along the side of the road. I slowed down to a cruise, watching them hop away. The trees gave way to the ocean's edge as I rounded a steep left turn and descended into a stunning bay of clear aqua waters. Waves were breaking everywhere.

'That'll do,' I said as I gravitated to the first wave I saw, getting my north confused with my south. Fighting waves of nausea, I pulled on my bikini and grabbed my 6'0" rainbow board, paddling out from a small boat ramp. As I neared the break I noticed that the waves were snapping onto the reef with terrifying force. Additionally, by my normal standards, the waves looked to be about ten foot. I looked down the line to see straight into a churning stand-up barrel.

'Shit.' I muttered. 'This is the *mellow* wave?' I sat right out on the shoulder and watched some bodyboarders free-falling down the face, knees and flippers in the air. Finally I gathered the courage to paddle for one and somehow managed to get to my feet and ride the last section of the wave. I paddled out further into the crowd to try my luck on one of the bigger ones, only to find myself cartwheeling down the face, pummeled by the thick lip down towards the shallow reef. I felt my foot hit so I pushed off, only to find myself still tumbling under water like I was in a washing machine, round and round. I scrambled for the surface in a panic but didn't make it before I felt the impact of another wave, and down further I went, lungs busting for air in the blackness. After what felt like about forty seconds (but was probably a lot less), I struggled to grab hold of my leg-rope and climb upwards to the surface, to finally gasp a lung-full of air. I scrambled as fast as I could onto my board to paddle towards the shoulder as oxygen slowly found its way back into my shaking limbs. I paddled back out knowing that if I didn't I'd feel defeated. Following another less intense wipeout I paddled back to my original position on the final section of the wave and took one more small wave back in towards the boat ramp, tail between legs.

All the same, I was giggling slightly as I lit a Sampoerna and leaned against the van. Much to my surprise, I heard my name.

'Hb?' I looked across to my left to see a friend from long ago parked right next to me.

'Jamie! What the hell are you doing here?'

'Looks like the same as you!' he responded in his friendly Canadian accent, giving me a big smile and a hug. I hadn't seen Jamie since we used to surf together with Stevie B in Byron Bay. As it turns out, Jamie was living at the top of the hill, and had been there for a while. Now I had a surfing buddy, sweet.

I got a couple of jobs. Somehow I ended up waitressing at 'Driftwood' Winery, and I also worked a couple of days in 'Satan's' shop, a general store right in the middle of the tiny town, named as such because everything was so expensive (and the owners name was Seaton). It was the only petrol station, food shop, newsagent, hardware store and center for alcohol provisions for miles, and when I worked there I was also the local postie and coastguard. Through the glass pie oven I could see North Point. I spent a lot of the quiet times writing poems and stories. I'd always wanted to write a book, and now I had something to write about. Every now and then the outside world would penetrate into my anonymity and a headline would show a terrified, screaming mother in Iraq, or the image of a bomb-site which would send me running into the cool room clutching my hand over my face as I tried to hold back the tears and grief.

During a flat spell, a couple of the local lads invited me to come skating with them, and they introduced me to the wonders of the big hill that rounded a corner up the top and wound its way down into the town. It was a perfect gradient to get loads of speed but still be able to carve and slow down if you needed to. I played with my speed, carving then crouching while enjoying the beauty of the bay and it's pristine crystal waters, hair streaming out behind me, sinking down into the tiny town I called home for this short, simple but beautiful time of my life.

I bought myself a 6'10" Aloha gun, which gave me the confidence I needed in the bigger surf. I took it out at Margaret River main break and finally back to North Point, one of the area's most challenging waves. After many unsuccessful attempts, I managed to catch a couple of decent waves on a solid day out there, waiting my turn to free-fall into some of the most incredible experiences of my life. I raced along the rushing wall of green water as the churning barrel threw the tube over my head and I dropped below sea-level in the skate-bowl section, pulling out with a sigh of pure ecstasy. As I started to tire I got lip-launched on my final wave, and when I came gasping to the surface in the impact zone I realised my board was gone. I swam with all my might towards the channel to stop the board from getting sucked back towards the peak, only to find the plug had been pulled right out of the board. North Point is *not* a normal wave. There was a single albatross surfing the wave that afternoon, gliding on the wave's air currents as the sky sank into sunset colours. I went home with salty skin and satisfied smile to pick up my oil pastels to paint the wave and the albatross.

Finally it was time to ask for help. Of course, I'd been asked countless times whether I wanted to see a counsellor, but I wasn't ready. But now, finally, in a place where I knew no one, I realised it was time. The silence, the runs on the empty coastline and the challenges that the ocean brought me each day were doing a great deal in bringing me closer to myself, but I knew there was still a long way to go. I found Valerie in Margaret River. She wore a dress of emerald green with shoulder length brown curls, and a smile that was younger than she was. By chance she was also an art therapist.

'I'm sorry, but what does that entail?' I asked, fascinated.

'Just bring in any picture you like,' she said simply. The only picture I had was the oil-pastel of North Point. Valerie viewed the picture approvingly and asked me a few questions. She pointed to the white bird, so I explained.

'Ever since Marc passed away, it feels as if his spirit is always close, especially in the ocean. At special moments, when I think of him, the birds appear. Sometimes they are in great flocks and they circle overhead and dance in the sky above me, and often times it is only one lone bird, especially when I surf by myself.' I remembered the albatross surfing the wave at North Point just days before.

Before I knew it I was producing more pictures. There was usually a small wooden boat with red sails. At first the boat was sailing away from a great castle, but soon found itself alone in a vast sea with heaving waves and no land in sight. After a while, Valerie suggested I draw a finger of land on the horizon. I drew a thin black line with a hint of green.

Soon the land was closer, a green hilly island. There was a lone figure in the bow. Before I knew it, she was standing on the shore, looking longingly out to sea. She had a very straight nose and long brown hair streaked with gold. She wore a regal dress of turquoise and there was a crown upon her head, but her eyes were very, very sad. Of course the woman was me, but I still felt very much as if I was bobbing helplessly on the open ocean. Where was my shore? Who was to place a crown upon my head? What was my destiny? I'd voiced the thoughts of millions to a world leader in the name of peace, yet the war was raging right then. Gunshots were flying, bombs were exploding, killing and maiming in just the same way they had in Bali. *Why* was the violence seemingly without end? I wandered down the main street of Margaret River and turned into a small bookshop with wooden doors. Running my hands across the books, feeling the spines pass under my fingers like ripples, I found a small green book and opened it to a random page.

'A rockpile ceases to be a rockpile the moment a single man contemplates it, bearing within him the image of a cathedral.' –Antoine de Saint-Exupery

I flicked through the pages and stopped on another quote:

'Often a crisis event explodes the illusions that anchor our lives.' –Robert Veninga

I walked over to the counter and handed the lady a twenty dollar note, tucking the precious little parcel under my arm as I walked back out onto the street.

'I can do this,' I whispered to myself. 'Whatever it is, I can do it.'

As the summer turned to winter the temperature started to drop and more and more big swells came rolling through, but I was getting used to it now. I took to swimming in the pool in Margaret River to further build my confidence in the water. I knew I needed to be super-fit if I kept on surfing bigger and bigger waves. Before too long I could easily do a couple of laps underwater and then I would swim a kilometre or so. More to the point, I was starting to go beyond merely surviving the takeoffs: I was learning to carve my way along the monster walls.

As it got colder still, a lot of people left town to take the long drive up to the tropical waters of Exmouth. Eventually, all the people who were left were basically big wave surfers, windsurfers and fishermen. Jamie stuck around and we enjoyed surfing some of the big swells with just us out sometimes. Everywhere I looked were gorgeous men: at the road works, behind the bar in Margaret River, in the bands that played, at the petrol station, even the check out dude in the supermarket. Everywhere! Too bad I never talked to any of them.

I loved WA, there was no doubt about that, but I was getting a lot of pressure from my family to come back, especially from Tommy. I felt I'd come a long way in those few months essentially by myself, but what was I ever going to do with half a degree? Could I really stay here and just surf big waves for the rest of my life? I really wanted to stay, but finally it was Gran's words that counted, small yet powerful over the phone:

'Are you going to finish your degree?' she asked.

I sighed and paused briefly. 'Of course!' I finally answered firmly, my decision made. I knew what it meant to her for me to finish this, so I booked my flight back East, and it was time for my last surf in the Indian Ocean.

Chapter 15

Back to Bali

I've been a long time alone now.
Who will hold me as I shake?
Who can warm me through the night?
Who will be there when I wake?
There was one once who loved me … a body soft
and warm.
Chilly winds blew, held me still through violent storms.
Soft breath whispered on my cheek.
Gentle heartbeat lulled me off to sleep.
It was a long time ago,
He held me when I shook with tears.
He warmed me through the winter,
But it's past tense now, with these passing years.
On a cold morning, we would wake.
Come on! He'd kiss me with a gentle shake.
As I rose, the engine running.
Into water we would plunge, laughing.
Green lines of water we would ride,

Ripples of the wind and tide.
Now tides have rose and tides have fell.
I rise alone, I drive alone, all moments by myself.
But it is still hard just sometimes, alone in the dark.
What is there to guide me to hear morning's lark?
Outside my window, waves crash on the shore,
Constant murmur of wild ocean's roar.
It's been a long time now that's passed me by.
Who can guide me to the light?
Who will hold me as I sigh?
These are lonely times … lonely nights.

THE BASALT HEADLAND of Lennox Point rises vertically out of the Pacific Ocean for hundreds of metres before it meets the green slopes that curve back down and around towards the town. A long, wide reef of smooth black boulders lines the shore, providing one of the best waves on the East Coast of Australia. I've lost a lot of fins and skin amongst the rocks at Lennox. There's a good scar on my left calf from one poorly timed slip off a barnacle-covered boulder as a wave washed up to my waist.

Lee found a place for us down in the town, sharing with him and one other fella. I took a look around the place, and sat on the dusty polished floor in the tiny room. A bushy hibiscus covered the window, with bright red flowers pushing against the screen. I sat there looking at the pale green walls thinking about my possessions and how they would fit in there: my redwood chest; my baskets; my trinkets.

How I would fit in to this room, and how Lennox Head would fit into my life.

It was a cold winter, the coldest I could remember in Australia. In the darkest hours of the night, as I struggled to sleep, the cold rose straight up through the thin futon on the floorboards straight into my bones. The southerly winds blew so strongly I imagined it entirely possible that freezing air from Antarctica itself was blowing straight into my bedroom with its rattling windows and no insulation. I was used to sleeping alone now, but a hot water bottle would have been very nice.

Surfing in the mornings before uni was a mission. We took it in turns to drag each other out from under the covers and into the cold, rusty old car. As the car heated we usually spent a long time checking the surf huddled in the warm procrastinating, before getting into a wet wetsuit and finally the salt water, which was actually a whole lot warmer than the biting southerly wind. If we managed to ease ourselves in the water before the wind picked up we would be rewarded with long crystal walls to carve together. Afterwards we took it in turns to jump under a hot shower, thawing our skin, peeling off our wetsuits and getting the blood flowing through our toes. We gulped down our tea and hot Weetbix sprinkled with brown sugar before dashing out the door as our first lecture started in Lismore, half an hour's drive away.

It was nice to be back at uni, back amongst the familiar faces, back in the lecture theatres and the labs; learning, talking, testing and taking it all in the best I could. Of course, there were a lot of sad, sympathetic expressions to get past for the first week or so. People were great, as one by one they acknowledged what had happened and shared their kind words with me; my fellow students, friends and lecturers. To be honest though, I'd usually duck straight into visit my Fairy Godmother Julianne. She ran a tiny shop in the uni Plaza filled with vintage clothes, brass candlesticks and her colourful paintings. She'd adopted me long ago when I'd come in crying before Marc and I had left Australia, and I was very glad of the refuge of her sweet-scented shop. I'd bring cake for us to share, hiding behind the glass counter drinking Julianne's delicious tea and reading our Angel Cards. I probably spent more time in there than I did in lectures.

Each day I went straight to the water; sometimes calm and clear blue and other days a mess of huge rolling whitewash. The ocean is never the same twice. It provided a pretty good metaphor for my life at the time. One moment I'd be sitting in a lecture with my peers, and in the next I'd pick up a paper to see my own face staring back at me. A day later I might be sitting in a spa with some Cornish mates under the Sydney Harbour Bridge, paid for by another media company keen to tell my story. Seemingly the next moment I would be back out in the surf and somehow remember that an assignment was due and I'd have to scramble my way up the rocks to frantically type away until the early hours. Some nights I spent alone with the door closed and my candles lit, tap-tapping my thoughts into my little silver laptop.

It was like having a little family for a while, coming home to a steaming meal on the round pine table as we took it in turns to cook big meals of veggies with plenty of cups of herbal tea on the go. The life I shared with Lee, Andy and other friends was pretty simple as we drifted from uni to the surf and back again. On the weekends I cracked a bottle of tequila as we climbed into whatever wacky clothes were appropriate to dance around at that particular themed party.

'Old age is for catching up on sleep!' was my catch-call as I poured another tequila for my friends, and they knew full well that I'd also be dragging them out in the ocean when the dawn hit. The southern end of Lennox has a Ti-Tree lake and after a surf we liked to dive into the tea-coloured water to freshen up, or to swim across into the deeper waters and dive into the freezing depths beneath the warm surface, coming up gasping for air.

One warm October evening I skated homewards alongside the beach at dusk, with the cicadas singing as loudly as the thoughts that were whirring in my head. Something in me was out of balance. Was it the bomb again? It had nearly been a year. I felt there were so many better reasons to be known than for surviving something so hideous, for the tragedy in my life. I would rather be known for doing something positive and making a real difference to the world, or at least for doing cool stuff like tackling huge waves. I gazed out at the ocean as it rushed past me, my hair streaming out behind me. I pushed harder, skating faster and faster.

I was to leave for Bali in a week. I hoped that amongst the sweetness and the richness, the dust and the sewers and humid Balinese air perhaps some answers might meet me there. At the front of my house I let the skateboard lose its speed and hopped off to stare at the crescent moon hovering over the headland. The horizon was glowing with the last red and orange of a sun that had long since set, the colours reflected on the calm dark waters of the bay. Finally, I decided I was looking forward to going back to Bali, but it wasn't going to be easy.

The morning before I was due to fly, I wandered about the house in a daze, thinking that maybe I should pack soon. It was mid-semester and I had plenty of uni work to do that I'd put on hold for the trip. It was hard to work on assignments when they felt so insignificant to me, and I was finding it difficult to focus on any one thing. Outwardly I was doing fine, but even the slightest scratch below my surface would reveal the babbling, lonely, sad mess of my ragged emotions. And I knew it had to get worse before it would get better.

Suddenly I was back in Bali, back on the Island of the Gods. It felt very strange arriving at the airport with Tommy to join the long queue to the passport check. I knew this was the beginning of my time to wade back into the dark, painful memories, and to start to heal. I could picture Marc just one year ago standing with his arms over his head in the teeming crowd outside the airport declaring, "I love this place!"

In Legian we stayed in a 'nice' hotel, but I would have rather been amongst the familiar faces of Legian Inn. I was not interested in air-conditioned rooms or lounging around by some chlorinated pool with a bunch of English and Australians. I wanted to get near to the Balinese, and somehow let them know that I shared in their grief over what had happened on their beautiful island home. As I ventured out, it was calming to hear the beep-beep of motorbike horns, the cars rushing by, the constant background noise of the Balinese chatter, to smell the rich smells and to see the bright colours everywhere. I heard the distant jingle-jangle of gamelan music, and remembered to expect a constant stream of ceremonies as I bumbled through the narrow winding streets and across the hot black sand beaches.

We hired a car so we could surf at Uluwatu, one of Bali's best but most crowded waves. I had a special '*I'm going for this wave and don't dare mess with me*' face, reserved just for Ulus. I made sure I caught a decent one early on and was careful never to pull back, so the men out there didn't assume they could drop in on me simply because I was a chick (but that didn't stop me from going over the falls from time to time).

On the third and fourth days the swell kicked right up and the crowds evaporated, so we paddled out on our guns to an almost empty lineup with maybe ten guys out. There was a lot of paddling to be done but we managed to navigate our way onto a few decent green walls. The cliff was lined with spectators and I was happy to notice that after the swell dropped off I still received a new level of respect from the local boys.

On the last day of the swell I was still surfing on my rainbow board but the legrope snapped and it got smashed on the reef. There was a moment I will never forget when I stood in knee-deep water as an eight-foot wall of water advanced. Just before it hit, someone behind the wave called out and asked me if I was okay, which gave me just enough time to make eye contact and laugh before I launched myself as high as possible and proceeded to bounce off the reef a few times. (A little bark lost but nothing that a drop of iodine couldn't fix). One of the Ulus locals, Made Lapur, agreed to fix up my board and let me borrow one of his little sticks for my afternoon surf. I caught a fast inside wave and was shocked at how light I suddenly felt through my turns, and the ease at which I could carve and weave from top to bottom on the green face. When I took it back I asked if I could buy it. With a smile and a shrug, Made obliged and sold it to me super cheap, which was how I discovered my Magic Board.

The next day was finally the twelfth of October. The ceremony was like nothing I'd ever experienced before, held at an enormous temple on the peninsular. A thousand people from all over the world gathered at the temple entrance where every one of them queued up the long white marble staircase towards the door where John Howard was standing. He shook every hand with a sympathetic, warm smile as they went through. As the queue crawled forwards, I must admit I had mixed emotions about shaking his hand for several reasons, particularly as it was the Australian government who had invited us to this occasion. As the moment came and went, I found it interesting that he noticeably looked the other way when his turn came to shake my hand, and he did the same to Tommy (there was no smile that's for sure). I took it as a compliment that he knew who we were.

The ceremony took place in the open air with a thousand seats laid out between two high walls, ornately carved with the best of Balinese stonework. Imposing statues of the Garuda (Eagle), the Barong, the Serpents and other Balinese gods had been carved out of massive white blocks of stone. Traditional Balinese dancing was interspersed with speeches by representatives from many countries and religions. It all came together to create a beautiful ceremony. As we heard them read out Marc's name amongst so many others, I looked to my left and realised that I had never seen Tommy cry before. He'd always tried to keep things together for the family. I guess he'd missed a lot of the ceremonies so far, including Marc's funeral. In my own misery I had forgotten how close they'd become. Tommy viewed Marc as a member of our family.

Only once did Howard refer to his 'war on terror' in his speech, which I had learned to expect, so on this occasion I chose to ignore it. Besides, it was too late now, the Iraq war was well underway. Following the ceremony we were invited to feast in a beautiful courtyard. Many familiar faces were present amongst the survivors and their families. At one point John Howard stood on his own not far from me, so I wandered over for a chat. First I thanked him for inviting us over, and then I started talking about how great it was that the US had just poured a chunk of money into education in Indonesia. This, I said, was a heartening approach, to seek peaceful and long-term solutions to the disparity and hatred against the 'Western' world. I took a sip of my water and paused, before making eye contact:

'So, Mr Howard, what are *you* doing?' As his eyes narrowed, I noticed they were markedly different to those of Blair. I could see a high level of intelligence, however the sadness I saw in Blair's eyes was not there, only a cold and calculated determination.

'Well…well,' he stammered, 'We already put 40 million dollars a year into aid into Indonesia.' As a lady approached us I nodded and thanked him, stepping away. That was enough, considering the occasion (still, I couldn't have let him get away completely scot-free either, especially considering he stood me up last time).

That evening thousands of people gathered on Kuta Beach, and Tim, Blaine and Bobby walked down with Tom and I. Bobby didn't really want to talk about it at all, and it broke my heart to see how he was holding the pain inside. Running and weaving through the crowd I found Christian, who I had not seen in a year. As we pulled back from a hug, I noticed that he looked exhausted and shaken. He told me that he had devoted many months to helping at Sanglah hospital after the blast, identifying the dead. I could clearly read the signs of grief and torment that he must have experienced. I led Christian to come and sit with the rest of us. Three thousand people from across the world sat on Kuta beach to light candles in remembrance of those lost and wounded in the Sari Club and Paddy's. Around me in the darkness I saw the whites of six thousand sad eyes. How could anyone on that beach ever forget?

On our last night we met with Bobby, Blaine, Tim and some other friends to eat Cornish pasties for dinner. This time we talked about anything but the bomb. The pasties were bloody good too, made by the Balinese to the recipe of a Cornishman's mother at a restaurant called the Secret Garden. No carrot in those Pasties!

Tommy and I took a special flight straight from Bali to the ceremony in Canberra to see the plaque where Marc's name will remain inscribed forever with eighty-nine others. The next day we were reunited with Carole, Ray and Steve, who had flown over from Cornwall for the occasion. Mum and Dad had caught the train from Byron, and so we all stayed together and went out for dinner. Marc would have been happy to see us all merrily enjoying each others' company, drinking West Australian wine in an Irish pub in Canberra.

In the morning the families assembled to catch an early bus to Parliament House. We were there to unite, quite possibly for the last time, with many of my fellow survivors. After the plaque had been unveiled, white doves flew up into the clear blue sky as a large crowd shuffled slowly in to the great hall. The ceremony unfolded with Christian hymns and prayers as the names of the dead slid slowly across a massive screen high above us with a white dove in the center. The politicians each spoke in turn, appearing suitably moved by the occasion.

John Howard stood behind a row of candles that sat in plastic tubs along the front of the stage. Just as he was optimising the opportunity to promote his ongoing war on terror, the candle flames started to join up. As Howard's speech reached its crescendo, the flames grew higher and higher, lighting up Howard's face with a strange red glow. I resisted the urge to run from the flames. When the plastic tubs began to catch alight, someone came in with a fire extinguisher and put them out. Although it was impossible to miss the irony, I realised this really was not the time for politics. It was an opportunity to face, acknowledge and release our feelings. Tears ran freely down the faces of Tom, Mum and Dad to my right, and Steve, Carole and Ray to my left. Our families, joined by Marc, were now lost without him. I looked beyond our group to see tears flowing on the faces of those all around; elderly and young alike; muscly footy players, politicians and priests, doctors and military. I realised at that moment how we are ultimately all the same.

I also realised the gift I had to take with me on this journey was the knowledge of what it is to love truly. But I was in no hurry. I was learning vital tools to help me on my way, to help me deal with pain, people, opportunities, life and the unexpected; whatever happened.

Chapter 16

Normal Life or Chaos?

I MAY NOT HAVE been in a hurry but life still seemed to be bowling along at breakneck speed. Towards the end of 2003, my friend Lian came from Granada in the Caribbean (where she was studying to be a vet) to visit me in Lennox Head. With exquisite timing, she arrived the moment I was on holiday. I took my exam in the morning and by the time I'd driven up to Brisbane airport to pick her up it was a sweltering November afternoon. Summer had arrived. I had freed up the whole month to spend with Lian, and we had one of the most carefree months of our lives, cruising around in the little gold Honda Accord I'd named the Star Car. The Star Car was a classic semi-automatic '79 model with three gears: *L* for Lift-off, *Star* for mystery adventure mode and *OD* gear for when everything just went a little odd. The stereo (controlled by The Navigator) mostly played 70s disco and Bob Marley. An excellent time was had as we explored the white-sand beaches and rainforest covered hills at the back of Byron

Bay, discovering stunning waterfalls and little cafes to stop for afternoon tea.

I gave Lian a full measure of Lennox student life, persuading her to drink tequila and dragging her out to a fancy dress 'school girls' party that raged for two days. She filmed me surfing at Lennox Point and took numerous photographs of our adventures. We cooked pasties for my family, chilled out at the Cove and went scuba diving at Julian Rocks. Another of my favourite people, Bobby, came over from America and we all went on a camping trip. It was great to catch some waves with Bobby on the empty beaches, and drag him out in fancy dress to a 'Boogie Nights' party.

'Do you think that maybe slowing down just a little bit might be a good idea?' Lian asked one day, as we zoomed towards our next adventure.

'What do you mean?' I asked. "There's just *too much* life to live. I feel like I've got to make the most of every moment. I've had the opportunity to live. Marc didn't. I'm not doing him or anyone who died any justice if I don't make the most of every day I'm blessed to live.'

'Okay, well maybe just slow down a bit in the car then,' she suggested quietly.

We climbed barefoot to the top of Wollumbin (or Mount Warning), the weathered plug of an ancient volcano in the center of the 'Turkey's Nest' caldera that stretches right out to Julian Rocks in the middle of the aqua waters of Byron Bay itself. We pulled ourselves up the chain right to the top and gazed out at the panoramic view of the green hills and the blue Pacific Ocean rippling out as far as the eye can see.

'You really live in Paradise,' Lian said.

'I know! Standing here, don't you just feel as if anything – *anything* you can dream of is possible?!'

'Anything,' she replied, her wide grin matching mine.

I took a quick trip to Sydney with my parents, and this time we went straight to Government House so Governor Bashir could award me with a Commendation for Brave Conduct. Jake Groneberg and Daniel Treacy had also come down from the Byron Bay area to receive bravery medals for pulling people out of the blast. The Governor was friendly and welcoming, inviting me back for afternoon tea at another time. As I held the golden feather and red ribbon in my hand, I couldn't quite believe that I deserved it. There was so much more I could have done – and people like Bobby and Blaine were just two more of so many unsung heroes that risked everything to help injured strangers in any way they could. If I could give my award to them, I would.

Soon, I was back in Bali with Tom, timed so we could witness the trial of the Bali Bombers. I took my first peek inside the new Paddy's, which bore an uncanny resemblance to the old one, music blasting, lights flashing, drunk tourists. But this time it had a very robust construction and lots of fire escapes. I had said many times that I could never go out again in Bali, but I went in there anyway to *make* myself dance. I guess the jungle juice helped. To tell the truth, I was petrified that something would happen to Tommy so kept a close eye on him (and the exits) the whole time. It was impossible to relax, but still out of (bloody stupid) determination (or belligerent defiance) I stayed on that dance floor under those flashing lights dancing to 'Land Down Under' for the millionth time. Hell, by the second jungle juice I was *almost* enjoying myself. Every Bali holiday I'd ever been on flashed through my mind, bringing back the innocent memories I'd gathered from many trips, but also following me were shadows of the nightmare. After a while, dancing there only served to help the numb and hollow feeling seep back into my heart and I left, crestfallen.

While in Bali I had a strange and vivid dream: I was walking on dry sand and came upon a cobra coiled up in a basket. Immediately the cobra jumped out and slithered towards me. As I was backing away I saw a deadly orange and black spider approach. They paused in front of me before attacking each other, then collapsed dead. A strong wind blew and within moments they had been covered in sand. As I awoke in the humid heat to watch the fan rotating above my head I wondered whatever could be next. Bounding out of bed, I decided to do something I had always wanted to do - I went out to order a suede Wonder Woman outfit to be tailor-made from my own design (I couldn't think of any reason why that would be a bad idea!).

Tommy and I took the inevitable trip to the dark Balinese courtroom, where the bombers were on trial. As I saw them standing there in front of me, I clutched onto the wooden railings between us, feeling a strange numbness and then a barrage of questions: Did these people *really* conspire to kill me, Marc and all those innocent people? Were these few men the ones responsible for destroying the innocence of a whole nation and changing the world for Australians forever? *Why?* Do they *really* have such a capacity for hate? What made them so different to *us*? What did it all *mean* and was this the end? Should they be shot and would that solve anything anyway? *Who's* law should we respect? I did not know. I had to steady and calm myself, focusing on the sound and the feeling of my heart slowly thumping in my chest.

On the final day, as I paddled out in the pink waves of an Uluwatu sunset, I started to ponder how much I loved Bali. Suddenly, it struck me that when the terrorists had struck I'd lost threefold: the man I love, my innocence, and my sanctuary, my escape, my Bali. Of course, since then my experience of Bali had changed but so had I. I loved surfing more than ever in Bali. On my Magic Board every wave was perfect! I had once said I could never party in Bali again, but I'd done it. And I had found *new* places to go, new things to eat, different ways of enjoying Bali. I'd made so many new friends, many of them Balinese, many surfers and travellers from across the world. It was wonderful to rediscover my love for Bali. It had become my home again. As I bobbed on the quicksilver waters of a perfect Uluwatu sunset, I made a conscious decision: As a tribute to Marc I would lead a wonderful life, grasping opportunities as I do the waves that come my way, to go for it with everything I've got, to ride them the best I can, and to love the journey along the way, wherever it may lead.

I headed down to Sydney for a few weeks. On my first weekend I'd booked in for the eye operation to treat my shortsighted vision (I'd always hated wearing glasses and contact lenses). The laser surgery hurt like hell (and they wouldn't give me any extra valium), but within just days I was no longer scared of losing my contact lenses, duck-diving with my eyes open to the rushing green. Every morning I awoke to see the world clearly, and whispered 'Thank you, Byron Bay!'

I had lined up work experience with a current affairs program on Channel 7. By now I'd carried out a hell of a lot of interviews with the media and wondered if I could use this experience to communicate environmental issues on TV. The work experience at Channel 7 opened my eyes to the other side of journalism as I tagged along to various interviews, answered their phone calls, dealt with story suggestions and shortlisted the interviews.

In the video archives, I was given access to footage of myself in Bali for the anniversary. I also saw somebody's footage of the Sari Club in full swing, and the front bar just before the bomb went off. My stomach felt heavy and sick as I saw Marc standing with his back to the bar watching us on the dance floor. The film angle came from near the entrance across the bar, from almost exactly where the bomb would have been. Marc was in full view, with nothing between him and the blast. I suppose it was better that way, somehow. At least it was further proof that his death was quick.

On my last weekend in Sydney I went to finally meet Tom Singer's family. They were such a lovely family and were coping well, but that didn't make it any less sad. I tried so hard to hold back the tears, but could not. I realised it would be the closest I could ever get to meeting Tom. I tried desperately to commit to memory all of the wonderful things they said about him. I could see that he had been much loved and a great kid, one who would never have the chance to be the man he aspired to be.

Back at uni, I'd taken an elective called Peace, War and International Politics. I'd never been so engaged in a subject. I read further into how Governments in the 'coalition of the willing' had been exposed for fabricating the case for war yet were facing no consequences, from the UN or from the people. How was this being allowed to happen? As my reading widened I learned more about how the media was used to polarize people and amplify fear (which I had experienced first hand through being misquoted on several occasions). My thirst for understanding was only growing as I learned more and more about the twisted web of associations and manipulation of the truth. I realised that war, politics, environmental destruction and big business were linked up *way* too much. All of this conflict was principally over an energy source that provided short-term gain for big business, at a massive cost to human life, culture and environment. The only gains to be made were in oil and reconstruction contracts, and weapons manufacture. Between long stints in the library I dived into the peace of Julianne's shop both to share my discoveries and to escape the overwhelming reality of it all.

I researched the Iraq War through books, newspaper archives and journals, and a series of interviews with ex-CIA agents, one of whom stated: 'The only strategic interest we have in the Gulf is oil.' I could now see that the war had been planned long before the Bali bomb. Already there was whispering that Iran was the next potential target. I'd never handed an assignment in early before.

There was another trip to Bali, and a boat trip to Sumbawa where I surfed some of the best waves of my life, flying down the face of a three hundred metre long wave of clearest turquoise above a multi-coloured coral reef. Time and time again I popped up from heavy wipeouts and pulled into aqua caverns of perfection, the ocean wearing away more of my pain's rough edges.

The second anniversary of the bomb came and went, only this time I chose to decline the media interest and sat alone on the dune in front of my house. To my horror, a picture of me on the dune featured in the Daily Telegraph, which I found pretty invasive, to say the least, to know that a photographer had been spying on me so they could get their money shot.

Bertha the Magical Mystery Machine was the name of my new, blue, VW van. I decked her out to my own design, dyed the curtains dark red and got a safe welded in under the passenger seat for my laptop and camera. Dad helped me insulate the roof and Julianne sewed up some cushions for the seats/mattress. I put a solar panel on the roof to power my fridge and fan. A selection of superheroes and a globe hung from the roof rack Tommy had made to hold up my shortboard, Marc's longboard, and my gun. In short, I was ready for anything! My final uni assignment was a short film I'd produced comparing culture and sense of place in Bali with Sydney. In my personal life it seemed I was pretty much ignoring my grief, while through my studies I was seeking to understand what had happened in any way I could, although it was entirely unconscious. Following the customary frantic rush down a university corridor to slip my final assignment in the box (with thirty seconds to go till deadline), I threw my stuff into Bertha and moved out of Lennox Head to take on a 12 hour drive down the Pacific Highway to Sydney.

I'd always wanted to spend a year living in a city, so I lived all over Sydney in Bertha. I started a job working as a 'Frontliner' for Greenpeace. I spoke to hundreds of people every day about how they viewed environmental issues. I loved the job and had a whole lot of faith in what we could achieve by working together for a good cause. My bosses quickly became great friends and our whole team became a tight social group, going out dancing to reggae music together. We also involved ourselves in some direct communications, making solar powered outfits; handing a wooden spoon award to delegates of a dodgy logging company; and jumping on the Greenpeace flagship, the Rainbow Warrior.

I parked Bertha in a different spot nearly every night, close to a beach and/or outside a mate's place. There was quite a crew of Aggie people who'd moved to Manly so I had a lot of fun going to BBQs and parties. For a while I dated a curly haired surfer boy from Mona Vale. I met some of the Sydney Greens and helped out with campaigns and traveled to state delegates' meetings. I was invited by a Peace group in Leichardt to speak at a public meeting of a few hundred people alongside 'Whistle Blower' Andrew Wilkie and Tim Anderson, a civil rights advocate who was falsely imprisoned for seven years on terrorism charges relating to the Sydney Hilton bombing of '78. The war was still going on, but it was old news so the papers mostly left me alone now.

I guess that I was now living a pretty normal life. I was happy, I loved my job, and I was surfing every day, but I don't think my feet were quite on the ground yet. One Saturday Andy came for a visit and we were on our way to a party with the Greenpeace crew. In haste, I skipped across a Sydney street without looking. Mid-skip, I was hit by a cruising taxi and managed to do a backflip over the top of it, bouncing off the windscreen and onto the road, head first. Miraculously, I was okay (but man, did my friends look scared). When I jumped up, Andy shook his head in disbelief as I apologised to the bewildered taxi driver.

I shot back up to Byron and Gran came over for my long awaited graduation. She kept clapping long after everybody else in the auditorium had stopped, a huge grin on her little face. It was wonderful to see Andy, Lee and so many uni friends walk onto the stage to receive their certificates. My degree felt like a huge achievement, and I had gained so much from my time at Southern Cross. If nothing else, the look of pride on Gran's face made everything worth it.

Soon, I was on the move again, driving back up to the Gold Coast, to manage the Greenpeace Byron/Gold Coast Frontline team. Then I started to travel to different parts of regional Australia to sign up members for Greenpeace. I was amazed at how happy people were to see us at little towns in outback Queensland. Certainly the people on the land seemed a lot more interested and aware of environmental issues than the folks in the city.

For Gran's 90th birthday, I drove to Byron to find my beautiful dainty Grandmother waiting for me. Gran and I spent a lot of time together exploring the fancy restaurants of the Gold Coast and Byron Bay. She hauled herself up into Bertha and we went on long drives through the hills, to waterfalls and stunning lookouts across the rainforests of the Border Ranges. We watched dolphins at play in Byron, as we stood on the little island overlooking The Pass. On the way back the tide had risen, so I carried Gran across the deeper water to set her down safely on the beach.

We cooked pasties together, which we now had down to a streamlined art. Gran made the pastry and rolled them out; I put in the filling and crimped them up; Gran basted them and put them in the oven. Here we were, Gran and I, separated by a generation and about as far from our homeland as it was possible to be, carefully assembling our traditional dish with love and care. There's nothing too remarkable that goes into a Cornish pastie, none of the individual ingredients are incredibly tasty on their own, but done right, in the right circumstances, shared with the right people, they are sublime. The whole is definitely greater than the sum of its parts. Andy came along to dine with the rest of us and it was a happy and rare feeling to have all the family together.

Often Gran and I just sat quietly together on the beach under the shade of a big rainbow umbrella with Beachie the dog, drinking a cup of tea and watching the waves. On one such occasion, just before she left, Gran turned to me to share some wisdom, speaking firmly:

'Always tell the truth, if there is only one thing you do,' she said, looking me straight in the eye. 'Oh, and try not to force things." She paused. "Is your Mother coming to Cornwall selling this summer?' she asked. 'I *wish* you were coming back on the plane with me.' And suddenly it clicked. Maybe I *could* go to Bali and buy stock to sell in Cornwall if Mum wasn't going to... Perhaps I could even keep going through Europe if I wanted... All I had to do was save enough to buy stock, a ticket and also... sell the van so I could buy another over there, and live in it too...

'Are you coming back to Cornwall this summer?' asked Gran again, her eyes fixed on me.

'Maybe Gran,' I replied. 'Anything is possible. Who knows?'

'Who knows, indeed?' she said, raising her eyebrows and her eyes to the sky before smiling back at me.

Epilogue

2012, THIRTY-TWO YEARS old. Where do I find myself now? Well, on the beach, of course. Very little appears to have changed, but my world has spun around many times since the day it was struck still, motionless, hovering and helpless until slowly but surely the momentum began to build, until it was spinning so fast I could barely grasp on to any memories to take with me. Thankfully, finally it's slowed down now, to a slow, steady spin, in line with the days, the months and the seasons of my life. So here I am, living in a beach shack (again) in Byron Bay, all my things finally dug out from cupboards, family lofts and corners, held together in bags and disintegrating boxes to now be laid out in colourful patterns about my home, telling a cryptic tale of the adventures of my life. I was gone for five years, and I've not been back long really, but long enough.

Things are good now.

They got pretty chaotic, but that's what happens when your deepest desire is to be as free as a girl can possibly be. Just before I left Australia, and just before I knew I was going to go, I went to Tasmania, popping by to catch up with Lee and his young family in Hobart. Waking up from a nightmare where I'd grown old overnight, I struggled to shake off the uneasy feeling as I reached for my little green book. I flicked through the pages and flipped it open about a third from the front, reading a short passage:

'Stop freewheeling, get into gear. There are many avenues to explore, so why not explore them? Never be afraid to step out into the unknown, into the new. Do it fearlessly, always expecting the best as you do so.' -Eileen Caddy

I didn't feel that it was a bad thing to grow old, not at all, but I realised that we must spend minimal time learning long, drawn out lessons and instead must move like a river, following that which is nearest and dearest to our hearts, our greatest desire of what we want to be and experience.

-Was I there now? Bali was now 44 months into my past, and I wondered what had I learned? -What had I experienced? What had it given me (-what had it taken?), -What had I accomplished since this time? When I drew back the years, which moments sprung out? What had given me the greatest enrichment for my soul? Importantly, was it the job I was doing now?

'No.' the answer leapt instantly and clearly into my mind.

'Okay, so what next?' came the reply.

I was restless, so I put on my joggers and started to run up the green southern hillside that overlooked Hobart. As my skin heated up in the crisp morning air, my fists were clenched as I ran up the steep slope, sending small rocks flying, keeping my focus on the ridge-line I could see high above me.

'I'll just make it to the top of this hill.' I muttered through clenched teeth, staring up as each foot landed in front of the other. Finally as the slope leveled off in a clearing I stopped. I looked out over the beautiful Tasmanian Landscape, the blue water and the green forest in the valley far below. As I turned a full 360 degrees I raised my eyes to the sky of brilliant blue, yet what I had failed to see was that right in front of me stood a towering mountain of stunning beauty, glowing in the morning sun. With the realisation that, had I not climbed the hill, I would never have known that the mountain existed, suddenly everything made perfect sense: it was finally time to move on.

I went travelling, bought a bomb of a car and drove around Europe for a while, sleeping under my boards. I caught some waves, drank a lot of Sangria, Portugese beer, absinthe, Vin Chaud, Italian Grappa and Scottish whiskey. I teetered and danced in car parks and cosy bars. I left my car under an olive tree in Portugal so I could head off to the Alps to learn to snowboard. I lived in France for a while, gliding off-piste under a clear blue sky, the only sound the creaking of my board in the soft snow, and the sound of my friends on the mountain slope below ... I lived on a community in Portugal, sleeping under the stars by a lagoon ... I stood on the most south-western tip of Europe overlooking the blue waters below, throwing my hands in the air. I was free as a girl can be. So, then what?

I drove home, back to Gran, and once more it was she who changed everything.

'When are you going to get a proper job?' she asked me quietly, but firmly.

'A job? Well... I'm still writing my book!' I replied smiling.

'What book?' she asked, raising her eyebrows. Ah yes, well, it was true I hadn't touched it in a couple of years now. Perhaps she had a point. I decided to stick around, Gran had been left on her own for too many years already.

I started off lifeguarding on the windswept Cornish beaches, but that sort of work runs out when it gets cold. I went to go for a swim at Truro College, but the pool was closed, so I wandered over the Uni building and filled in some paperwork to do a post-grad teaching course. Before I knew it, I was in front of a class of students and found myself loving it. I dressed up in the appropriate smart clothing, (which felt like fancy dress at first) learning the nuances of the role, in particular that a hungover teacher doesn't do the kids any justice, so I started to become slightly more sensible, responsible even. Slowly but surely my chaos became organised. It had to be. Gran had fallen ill and needed me more than ever, so I took her food each day and tried my best to see to it that she had everything she needed. When she got a little better we went out driving through the countryside. It was a familiar sight to see us sitting by the flowers outside a sunny Cornish pub, a glass of cider to drink with our fish lunch. Slowly but surely, though, I watched Gran fade away. At least her passing was in the right order this time, which is easier to handle.

Determined to make the most of my sedentary life, I ticked my dreams off one by one. I sailed on the rivers of Cornwall; I learnt to play guitar and sing, I even wrote and recorded songs, eventually finding myself up on stage. I went on mystery tours, adventuring through the lanes, finding a tiny gramophone shop tucked away on a cliff top, as if hidden from time itself. I visited castles and ancient megaliths that had been there before the Celts. I visited new and old friends regularly, sitting by cozy fires all around Cornwall. I saw a fair bit of Carole and Ray, who were busy travelling here and there in their camper van. I plunged into community life in the village of my birth, my ancestry. I learnt what it was like to be on committees, to discuss improvements to the village, to try to get things moving for young people, finding myself in a number of roles. I kept working at the college, and by the time three years were through I found myself lecturing in Sociology and World Development, and running much of the Environmental Science course. But I still skated to the beach.

As for men? Of course you ask that question, so let's get it out of the way. Well, I'm still alone. Call it long-term single.

Yes, sure there were a couple of hopefuls (well *I* was hopeful at least), but inevitably they faded away, like a set rolling through too much water, a green wave-crest rising up with the promise of the perfect ride. As excitement builds, you paddle like hell, only to see the wave drop and slump as it hits deep water, just another line of swell moving through, past and gone. With their passing were tears, questioning, growth, and even bursts of frustration, anger and bitterness. I feel that when it comes to affairs of the heart, no promise can ever be made fully, for one thing we cannot plan for is the rise and fall of our own desire.

Regardless, some beautiful moments were shared, and really that's what life is made up of isn't it? Moments. That's what makes them so special, the unique place and time, the circumstance, the sun overhead, the lapping waves on the shore, the footsteps in the sand, or on the dancefloor. None of it will ever be quite the same again, coming together with the same sequence of events. Those experiences may be the jewels placed in the crown of our destiny, but I've discovered there is nothing permanent nor continuous in such moments.

But there's always been *real* waves to ride, smiles, friends and adventures, so I can't complain. I love the days when Lennox Point sends through it's perfect rolling lines of green. In fact, I bought a board especially for it, called the silver bullet, I don't want to miss my chance to ride the next big swell.

It's not *all* about the waves any more, though. I can go for a few days without surfing. I run, I swim, I do my yoga. I meditate most days and when it's flat I don't care. In fact, I love to put on my Balinese cone-hat and head for the open ocean to chase whales on my stand-up paddle board, coming back to shore to explore coves, rivers, lakes and hidden beaches, jumping off and swimming around the rocks with my flippers. I don't drink much any more, and smoking doesn't really do it for me either. I still love to dance, more than ever. In fact, I'm learning to Salsa (although I haven't yet managed to graduate from the beginners' class). It's a good lesson to relinquish control and allow oneself to be led for just one hour a week.

I called Ray just yesterday. He and Carole were drinking tea in a beautiful Cornish garden overlooking Crantock, a beach Marc loved to surf. Ray's playing music again. Ten years ago he vowed to never play again, but last night he said he was playing better than ever. He's nearly 75. Age doesn't seem to be much of an obstacle these days, especially when you're determined to make the most out of every day like Ray. Steve, Marc's big brother has finally had his first child. I went to visit them earlier this year, holding little Jonty Marc in my arms, with tears of joy, and sadness rolling down my face.

Closer to home, in fact just around the corner are my own parents living in the house Tommy (and Dad) built. As for Mum and I, well... peace in your own family can be one of the greatest challenges of all. Although our family is never going to be perfect, there's a whole lot of love there. At 71 years, following a heart attack, Mum still surfs most days on the perfect waves of The Pass. She's also learning to dance Salsa and play guitar. When I'm really busy she'll bring round a nice vegan wrap to sit down with me for lunch. Dad still has a thick head of hair and a busy moustache, we wander around the Byron Markets together each month. They still go to Bali together every year.

I guess it's safe to say that, generally, I have a lot more control over my life these days. You could even say I've got a pretty firm hold of the reigns. I'm still at Uni, would you believe it? It's different this time though. I actually work pretty hard. I *do*! I teach there now, but yes, I am still studying, for a PhD this time (I can't bear the idea of staying a Miss or a Ms forever!).

There's a new issue sweeping through the hills and countryside of Australia's back yards. I found out about it when it was still unknown to most. I watched a film, Gasland, and it changed my life. Ever curious, I had to find out what was going on, and get to the bottom of it if I could, finding out about large-scale gas developments happening all across Australia, in fact across the world. What concerned me the most was that it seemed to be risky for the environment, and it seemed to be happening largely without community consultation.

I put together my experiences in Cornwall and at Greenpeace to work with community groups, helping them come together. I worked on communication tools for helping groups to get focused and organise themselves better (ironic, hey). An issue like that brings together a lot of passionate people, and they sometimes get lost and understandably emotional. Coming from a scientific perspective, I do what I can to remove the emotion and focus on the topic in hand and on what needs to be done to get things rolling.

At the core of it all, it comes back to peace. Like a dictatorship that is overthrown by an angry group, more of the same is likely to come eventually. But if every step of change comes from peace, from integrity, openness and truth (and even *fun*), then surely a model can exist for this on a larger scale? But if it is not apparent in the individual, then how can it be expected to exist in the whole? Peaceful change can't be forced. It starts inside, and like a smile, has the potential to ripple out to all corners of the earth.

I picked up my pen, and with a little help from my friends, I wrote my story. It took a while to get the ink flowing but, like most things, once you get started it's not so bad. I'd learnt a bit of focus along the way and this, coupled with the determination I've picked up, made for a relatively smooth journey. Of course, there's a few dark secrets hidden in here. I've done my best to give them as much light as possible, extracting them from the rat-chewed boxes. I've tried to give them order. -Some things are easier to deal with than others. There was a box overflowing with newspaper clippings. I spent days reading through, ordering them into plastic folders, then putting them away again.

Where is Marc in my life now? At a glance, I see him right here. His purple guitar is hung up on the wall, his green long-board still finds itself often under my feet. Of course I wish he could be here to meet the lively, joyous friends that I spend my days with, to sit and play music with us, to paddle out with us, but that's not our fate.

So here I stand strong, central, rooted in life, connected to the earth, while living each day, riding each wave as it comes, the barrel spinning around me, yet for an instant I am still, like the axel of a wheel. After this long journey, at my center I can say there is peace, like the clear waters of a deep, still lake.

And, finally, I am free.

Have you heard about the Peace Pledge?

It's an independent movement to encourage and support people as they strive for greater peace in their daily lives, resulting in more peaceful communities.

Originating in Sydney, Australia, (Bondi Beach actually!) but with reach into the USA, UK, Asia, Europe, United Arab Emirates, South America, Africa, India and Pakistan, and more, it is part of a global consciousness movement with the aim of helping human beings reach their full potential, and ultimately achieve social harmony.

The idea is that through a commitment to personal peace, World Peace comes one step closer. From small seeds, big trees grow.

The vision for Peace Pledge is to attract five million pledgers, people prepared to not just take the Pledge but to honour it in their daily lives.

Perhaps after we hit the five million mark we'll double the goal to ten...

You see, there won't be peace on Earth till there is peace in the heart of every man, woman and child... so could you help us get the word out? Tell your friends!

If you'd like to know more about the Peace Pledge, contribute in some way, or make a donation please email: info@thepeacepledge.org
We would love to hear from you.

Want to read the Pledge? Please take a look at the website or visit the Facebook page.

World peace begins with you - will you take the Pledge?

www.ThePeacePledge.org

www.facebook.com/peacepledge

Lightning Source UK Ltd.
Milton Keynes UK
UKOW032211091012

200302UK00002B/1/P